Empowered Parenting

Raising Kids in the Nurture and Instruction of the Lord

Robert J. Morgan

LifeWay Press
Nashville, Tennessee

ISBN 0-8054-9815-X
Dewey Decimal Classification: 649
Subject Heading: CHILD REARING\PARENTING

This book is the text for course CG-0202 in the subject area
Home/Family in the Christian Growth Study Plan.

Unless otherwise noted, Scripture quotations are from the Holy Bible,
New International Version
Copyright © 1973, 1978, 1984 by International Bible Society.

Verses marked TLB are taken from *The Living Bible*. Copyright ©
Tyndale House Publishers, Wheaton, Illinois, 1971. Used by permission.

Scripture quotations identified as CEV are from the *Contemporary English Version*.
Copyright © American Bible Society 1991, 1992. Used by permission.

Scripture quotations marked GNB are from the *Good News Bible*, the Bible in
Today's English Version. Copyright © American Bible Society 1976. Used by permission.

Scripture quotations marked NASB are from the *New American Standard Bible*.
© The Lockman Foundation, 1960, 1962, 1963, 1968, 1972, 1973, 1975, 1977.
Used by permission.

Printed in the United States of America

LifeWay Press
127 Ninth Avenue, North
Nashville, Tennessee 37234

To my parents

John I. Morgan
Edith Morgan

Both still living—

One on earth
and one in heaven.

Meet
Robert J. Morgan

Robert J. Morgan is senior pastor of the Donelson Fellowship, Nashville, Tennessee. He and his wife, Katrina, have three teenagers—Victoria, Hannah, and Grace; and three sheep, two dogs, and a cat. Reverend Morgan is a graduate of Columbia Bible College, Wheaton Graduate School, and Luther Rice Seminary. His writings have appeared in magazines like *Leadership Journal, The Christian Reader, Aspire, Focus on the Family, Decision, Experiencing God Magazine,* and *Moody Magazine.* He is a frequent contributor to *ParentLife* and *Living with Teenagers.* In addition to *Empowered Parenting,* Reverend Morgan has written a children's devotional book, *Tiny Talks with God* (Thomas Nelson, 1996), and a Christian apologetic, *Beyond Reasonable Doubt* (Evangelical Training Association, 1996). He is an effective conference and retreat speaker and has ministered in Asia, Africa, and Latin America as well as across the United States. He is available for speaking engagements. For scheduling information, contact Cool Springs Artists and Speakers, Inc. at 615-771-6644.

Contents

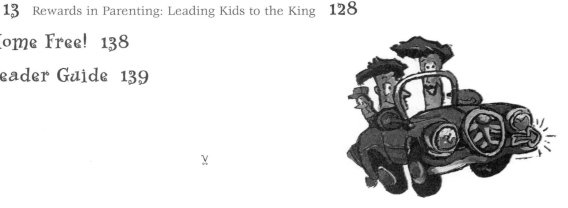

Introduction

Trippin' into the 'hood?

Parenthood?

Great! Here's a simple guidebook—small *g*—for your trip. The parenting journey is fun, fearful, and sometimes frantic. It winds along mountain ridges and through shadowed valleys. It sometimes jigs and jags in unexpected ways. Yet it generally follows some observable routes, and an experienced guide can often offer timely advice.

The real Guidebook—the one with the capital *G*—is the Bible. We'll begin our trip by getting our bearings from Scripture's foundational text on parenting, Deuteronomy 6:5-7. This passage comes early in Scripture, and that is where we will start.

Then we'll begin our trek on home turf by looking at three types of home settings. As we consider the traditional family, we will focus on the primary relationship in the home—the one between husband and wife. A good marriage facilitates the parenting trip, so it is important to understand how good marriages develop. What do you do when the marriage isn't so good? Or when there's no marriage at all in the single-parent home? And how do you step into stepparenting or blended-family living? The Bible has some answers for us and guides us no matter what our home turf is like.

I'll assume the job of tour guide. In broad terms I will tell you what to expect around the curves and over the hills as we look at the stages in the journey—from pregnancy to adolescence.

The last half of the book will deal with signposts and speed bumps we encounter along the way: basic parenting issues that you're bound to face or that you're facing right now. These include discipline, fatigue, the value of Scripture memory, when your children break your heart, and the satisfaction of children making a commitment to Christ.

Along the way, look for features like Bible Search, Let's Talk, and Practical Suggestions. These are identified by mail boxes and traffic signs. When you come to one of these, pause and do what it asks. You will gain much more from your study if you do.

For group study, material can be read in advance, with a facilitator presenting a brief summary of the content before guiding the group in its discussion of the material. We have included group suggestions beginning on page 139.

The learning map included with this book provides an overview of the entire course and will serve you well as you journey through the material. It will also be helpful in group sessions.

I need to make one confession from the beginning—I'm a little scared. I can't think of anything more frightening than writing a guidebook for parents. Parenting is intimidating enough; telling others how to do it is downright dangerous. As the father of three children, I can identify with John Wilmot, the Earl of Rochester, who once quipped, "Before I was married, I had three theories about raising children. Now

I have three children and no theories."[1] The late actor Telly Savalas put it more bluntly: "Makin' em is easy," he said. "Raisin' em might be a little tough."[2]

As you journey into the 'hood, remember that while the Bible's advice is infallible, mine isn't. I've been a highly imperfect dad, and I have the stories to prove it. Several years ago, for example, my middle daughter, Hannah, was being stubborn at breakfast. She didn't want milk on her cereal. I doused it with milk anyway. Hannah dug in her heels, refused to eat or touch it, and even refused to look at it. A little whirlwind swirled inside me that within 30 seconds became a full-blown twister.

"Eat the stupid cereal!" I screamed. For emphasis, I grabbed her cereal bowl, raised it over my head, and threw it to the floor with all my strength. It exploded, shattering into a thousand pieces, milk and cereal splattering everywhere. My wife screamed, and the girls fled to their rooms. The cat climbed the curtains. And our little dog laughed (I think) to see such a sight.

This incident was particularly upsetting because the clerk at the department store had told us the china was unbreakable!

But it wasn't, and neither is a child's heart. We can damage their spirits very quickly.

I immediately felt remorse. As soon as our family regained a semblance of composure, I went to my daughter's room, sat on the bed, and apologized. That day I learned children can accommodate imperfect parents if we're sincere, humble, and willing to admit our mistakes. Shouldn't we treat our kids with the same politeness we'd show perfect strangers? We're often quick to say, "Pardon me," "Excuse me," and "Please forgive me," when offending a passing acquaintance. Should we do less for our own children? We aren't perfect parents; we're going to bungle the job occasionally. That's when we need to apologize and ask for forgiveness.

So, I've made my confession and in so doing I've established the theme of this book: God is the only perfect Parent and the Bible is the only perfect Guidebook. *Empowered Parenting* will be helpful only as it channels God's insights into your journey through the 'hood.

The apostle Paul put it another way in 2 Corinthians 12:9. Paul teaches us that God's work, including parenting, must be done in His power, for we're too weak and foolish to do it on our own: "My grace is sufficient for you, for my power is made perfect in weakness." A chapter later, he added, "He [Christ] is not weak in dealing with you, but is powerful among you. For to be sure, he was crucified in weakness, yet he lives by God's power. Likewise, we are weak in him, yet by God's power we will live with him to serve you" (2 Corinthians 13:3-4).

I pray this book will help you find in Jesus Christ and God's Word strength for the journey and empowerment for effective parenting.

---

[1] John-Roger & Peter McWilliams, *Do It! Let's Get Off Our Buts* (Los Angeles: Prelude Press, 1991), 175.
[2] Ann Trebbe, "'Kojak' Is Back on the Mean Streets," *USA Today*, 3 November 1989, 2D.

Getting Your Bearings

Three Habits of Spiritually Empowered
Parents

∾ 1 ∾
Three Habits of Spiritually Empowered Parents

The old man grabbed his well-worn staff and with a grunt pushed himself to his feet. He was only days from death, yet he managed to stand and address his audience of young adults. His reputation as a popular writer and speaker stemmed from the four bestsellers he had already written. Now he was finishing his fifth and final volume, delivering it orally to the young parents who sat at his feet.

The author's previous books had described one tragedy after another stemming from powerless parenting. In his fifth book, he was giving his audience a set of secrets, garnered over a lifetime of observation, to enable them to avoid the mistakes he described in previous volumes.

He was telling them how to be successful parents.

The old man was Moses, and his previous books—Genesis, Exodus, Leviticus, and Numbers—we now call the first four books of the Bible. His fifth book, delivered verbally to the new generation just before they entered the promised land, is Deuteronomy.

Parents "UnAbel" to Raise Cain

Moses described the first troubled home in history. Adam and Eve raised a boy named Cain, the first person to enter the world through a woman's womb. For awhile there were only three. Then Adam and Eve had another son, Abel. The two brothers frolicked and fought as boys do. They went to church together. That is, they both worshiped God.

That's where the trouble started.

Scripture Search: Read Genesis 4:1-8.

Adam lay with his wife Eve, and she conceived and gave birth to Cain. She said, "With the help of the Lord I have brought forth a man." Later she gave birth to his brother Abel.

Now Abel kept flocks, and Cain worked the soil. In the course of time Cain brought some of the fruits of the soil as an offering to the Lord. But Abel brought fat portions from some of the firstborn of his flock. The Lord looked with favor on Abel and his offering, but on Cain and his offering he did not look with favor. So Cain was very angry, and his face was downcast.

Then the Lord said to Cain, "Why are you angry? Why is your face downcast? If you do what is right, will you not be accepted? But if you do not do what is right, sin is crouching at your door; it desires to have you, but you must master it."

10

Now Cain said to his brother Abel, "Let's go out to the field." And while they were in the field, Cain attacked his brother Abel and killed him.

What was Cain's root problem? ✔ Check one.
❑ Emotional: He took everything personally.
❑ Spiritual: He had a problem with God.
❑ Psychological: He had low self-esteem.
❑ Social: He did not get along with others.

Moses made it clear that the problem in Genesis 4 was not primarily emotional, though emotions were involved. It wasn't primarily social, though destructive social patterns developed. Nor was the problem psychological, though great deficiencies riddled Cain's personality. The root problem was spiritual. Cain's relationship with God was faulty, and this spiritual deficiency led to jealously, anger, depression, and violence.

Cain's root problem caused a chain reaction. Below are several links in the chain. Using the numbers 1 through 6, put the links in the order that seems most appropriate to you.

__ Depression   __ Anger
__ Separation from God __ Resentment of his brother
__ Murder   __ Faulty worship

Faulty worship led to anger, which led to depression, which led to separation from God, which led to resentment of his brother, which led to murder.

If you could have counseled Cain, which of the following verses would best describe your starting point? ✔ Check one.

❑ "We should love one another" (1 John 3:11).
❑ "Starting a quarrel is like breaching a dam; so drop the matter before a dispute breaks out" (Proverbs 17:14).
❑ "Blessed are the peacemakers, for they will be called sons of God" (Matthew 5:9).
❑ "Repent, then, and turn to God" (Acts 3:19).

Why did you select that verse?

_____

Abraham

With a slow, sad shake of his head, Moses turned from that story to tell us others. In Genesis 12 he introduced a family whose story forms the backbone of Old Testament history—the family of Abraham. Abraham was a tower of faith, repeatedly cited in the New Testament for the solidarity of his trust in God. The Bible says, "Abram believed the Lord, and he credited it to him as righteousness" (Genesis 15:6).

Paul offered the best definition of faith in the Bible when, referring to Abraham, he wrote, "He did not waver through unbelief regarding the promise of God, but was strengthened in his faith and gave glory to God, being fully persuaded that God had power to do what he had promised" (Romans 4:20-21).

Faith is the persuasion that God has the power to do what He has promised. Abraham's example teaches that. The writer of Hebrews echoes Paul's tribute to this giant, "By faith Abraham, when called to go to a place he would later receive as his inheritance, obeyed and went, even though he did not know where he was going" (Hebrews 11:8).

Yet Abraham had a flaw in his faith, a blind spot that was passed from father to son until it nearly destroyed his posterity.

Genesis 12 begins with God's promise to Abraham: "I will make you into a great nation" (v. 2). But in the very next paragraph, Abraham doubted God's ability to keep him alive long enough to father a child. In Egypt, he resorted to lying to protect himself from being murdered because his wife, Sarai, was ravishingly beautiful; and Abraham envisioned himself being killed by someone wanting her. Despite God's promise a few verses before, Abraham questioned God's ability to keep him and he deteriorated into a deceiver.

As he was about to enter Egypt, he said to his wife Sarai, "I know what a beautiful woman you are. When the Egyptians see you, they will say, 'This is his wife.' Then they will kill me but will let you live. Say you are my sister, so that I will be treated well for your sake and my life will be spared because of you" (Genesis 12:11-13).

The Bible tells us that this deception was an ongoing practice. Abraham routinely deceived the people around him, wherever he went. Years before, when leaving Ur of the Chaldeans, he had conspired with Sarai, "When God had me wander from my father's household, I said to her, 'This is how you can show your love to me: Everywhere we go, say of me, "He is my brother"'" (Genesis 20:13).

What happens when a child sees a persistent compromise in his father's character? What impact did this flaw have on Abraham's son, Isaac? Isaac saw his father's faith at its best on Mount Moriah (Genesis 22). But he saw it at its worst, too, and the flaw was passed on to him.

He became just like his dad.

Isaac and his beautiful wife, Rebekah, traveled to the land of the Negev. "When the men of that place asked him about his wife, he said, 'She is my sister,' because he was afraid to say, 'She is my wife.' He thought, 'The men of this place might kill me on account of Rebekah, because she is beautiful'" (Genesis 26:7).

 Let's Talk: **In what sort of spiritual or religious environment did you grow up?**

The trend doesn't stop with Isaac and Rebekah. They raised a boy named Jacob who grew up seeing both his father and grandfather weave a thread of deception into the fabric of their faith.

The result? Jacob's very name came from the Hebrew verb meaning "to deceive." No other man in the Old Testament bore this name, and Jacob lived up to it. He spun webs of deceit throughout his youth, the worst being the duplicity he practiced against his own father by stealing his brother's blessing (Genesis 27).

The result? Jacob had 12 sons whose descendants formed the 12 tribes of Israel. The sons became ruthless liars who sold one brother into slavery. They told their aged father that Joseph had been killed by a wild animal, and for two decades they stuck by their cruel deception.

Like father, like son, and grandson, and great-grandson.

No wonder Moses commented in his next book, Exodus, that God punishes "the children for the sin of the father to the third and fourth generation of those who hate me" (Exodus 20:5).

Leviticus, Moses' third book, relates another tragic like-father-like-son story. Moses' brother Aaron, the high priest of Israel, was a good man whose faith, like Abraham's, harbored a blot at its core. At Mount Sinai he had molded an unauthorized idol in the form of a golden calf for the people to worship. It isn't totally surprising, then, that we find a similar pattern in his sons, Nadab and Abihu.

> *Aaron's sons Nadab and Abihu took their censers, put fire in them and added incense; and they offered unauthorized fire before the Lord, contrary to his command. So fire came out from the presence of the Lord and consumed them, and they died … (Leviticus 10:1-2).*

Moses' fourth book, Numbers, is peppered with rules and regulations concerning family dysfunction. Moses described the total parental breakdown of one generation of Israelites, resulting in 40 years of wandering in the wilderness.

 Let's Talk: **Have you detected any negative patterns in your life or relationships that you picked up from your parents? How can you prevent their being passed on to your children?**[1]

Deuteronomy

From the garden of Eden to the desert of Sinai, Moses chronicled the devastation of failed families. Now he wanted to help a new generation of parents preparing to enter the promised land. They were ready to raze Canaanite cities for God. But Moses was more eager for them to raise Israelite children for God. In Deuteronomy 6, he uttered a series of statements that became the Jewish *Shema*, the most honored passage in the Old Testament for Jews. It begins with "Hear, O Israel: The Lord our God, the Lord is one" (Deuteronomy 6:4).

The verses that follow bestow the best advice about parenting found in all of human literature. Three sentences summarize every good word that has been spoken on the subject of effective parenting. Deuteronomy 6:5-7 describes the three habits of spiritually empowered parents. "Love the Lord your God with all your heart and with all your soul and with all your strength. These commandments that I give you today are to be upon your hearts. Impress them on your children."

Habit 1: Empowered Parents Love the Lord Deeply

Empowered parents love the Lord their God more than anything else— even their children. Jesus said, " 'Seek first his kingdom and his righteousness, and all these things will be given to you as well' " (Matthew 6:33). Where do you find the wisdom you need for raising children? Where do you get the joy and patience? Where does the love and compassion come from? '

All the emotional and psychological resources we need for child rearing flow from our relationship with Christ. And if we try to cultivate our relationship with our sons and daughters without cultivating our relationship with God's Son, we'll build a house of sand. Your friendship with your kid will never be greater than your fellowship with God.

I sometimes ask this question to groups I'm addressing: What is the worst sin possible to commit?

Genocide?

Infanticide?

Rape?

Torture?

No. The answer is surprisingly simple. The greatest sin is breaking the greatest commandment. What, then, is the greatest commandment? A lawyer posed that question to Jesus. Christ answered by quoting from the *Shema*: " 'Love the Lord your God with all your heart and with all your soul and with all your mind.' This is the first and greatest commandment" (Matthew 22:37).

The gravest sin we can commit, then, is breaking the greatest commandment: loving anything more than God.

 Let's Talk: **Most Christians struggle with the issue of "full surrender" at various points along their spiritual journeys. What do you think "full surrender" means? Is there an idol in your life that stands between you and full surrender to Christ?**

Scripture Search: **Read the following verses:**

Therefore, I urge you, brothers, in view of God's mercy, to offer your bodies as living sacrifices, holy and pleasing to God—this is your spiritual act of worship (Romans 12:1).

"You shall have no other gods before me" (Exodus 20:3).

"But seek first his kingdom and his righteousness, and all these things will be given to you as well" (Matthew 6:33).

All these verses tell us to ... (put in your own words) ...

_____

_____

Relate the above verses to Proverbs 14:26:

He who fears the Lord has a secure fortress,
    and for his children it will be a refuge.

What does it mean to "fear" the Lord? How does "fearing the Lord" provide security for our children?

_____

_____

    Idolatry is letting something come before Jesus in your life. And that includes your kids! In fact, Christ's words in Matthew 22 are directly related to Genesis 22, the story of Abraham's relationship with Isaac.

    Despite the flaw in his faith, Abraham harbored a burning devotion to the Lord. All of his life, he loved God. But when in his old age he fathered a child, God tested him to see if his love for Isaac had eclipsed his love for God. Notice how persistently the Lord made His point: "Take your son, your only son Isaac, whom you love, and go to the land of Moriah. Sacrifice him there as a burnt offering" (Genesis 22:2). God left no doubt as to His motive for the test, describing Abraham's boy in four different ways: your son, your only son, Isaac, the son you love.

    Abraham proved obedient, and just before the knife fell an angel stopped his hand, saying, "Don't hurt the lad in any way, for [now] I know that God is first in your life" (Genesis 22:12, TLB).

Is God first in yours?

Habit 2: Empowered Parents Study the Bible Daily

The second habit of empowered parents is found in the sentence following the *Shema:* "These commandments that I give you today are to be upon your hearts" (Deuteronomy 6:6).

If you want to be a good parent, spend time with the Bible and layer your heart with God's Word.

Read and study it.

Memorize its verses.

Meditate on them day and night.

One of the things that deeply impressed me as I grew up was my father's love for the Bible. He was raised at the top of a mountain in East Tennessee, a mile or two from the nearest road. His father died when he was only seven. About all he remembered of his dad was his funeral and the rain beating on the tin roof of a shed near the cemetery. But somehow, a few years later, my dad walked out of those Appalachian mountains, attended the University of Tennessee, became an educator, and spent his life helping young people.

His secret? He loved his Bible.

Late at night, I'd crawl out of bed to go to the bathroom or to get a drink of water, and there he'd be in the den of our home, reading his Bible. Week after week I'd listen to him discuss the Bible with his older brother, who was also a keen student of Scripture. Year after year he taught a men's Bible class at the church we attended.

He bought me my own Bible when I was just a small boy, and his example taught me to love it. There has never been a truly effective, empowered parent in the history of the human race who neglected the infallible, beautiful, practical Word of God.

My friend Anne Worthington recently told me about her parents. Despite educational limitations, they mastered God's Word. "As long as I can remember," she said, "they rose at 5:00 in the morning to spend an hour in Bible study and prayer. When my father was employed, he got up at 4:30 to study and pray. As long as I live I will remember hearing him in the bathroom praying out loud over his prayer list, even one time when we went to visit an aunt. I can remember being so embarrassed on that occasion."

"Now," she adds, "at age 84 they still hunger and thirst for God's Word." Their example whetted Anne's appetite for the Lord.

Ruth Bell Graham, wife of evangelist Billy Graham, treasures similar memories. "Each morning when I went downstairs to breakfast, my father—a busy missionary surgeon—would be sitting reading his Bible. At night, her work behind her, my mother would be doing the same.

"Anything that could so capture the interest and devotion of those I admired and loved the most, I reasoned, must be worth investigating. So at an early age I began reading my Bible and found it to be, in the words of the old Scotsman, 'sweet pasturage.' "[2]

John G. Paton of Scotland pioneered missionary work to the South Pacific a hundred years ago, and his story is movie material. What inspired Paton's staunch devotion to God? He grew up in a quaint cottage with a roof of thatch and walls of stone. There were three rooms. The first was a combined bedroom, parlor, and kitchen. The rear room was a work room filled with stocking-frames. The middle room was a bare little place with only space for a bed, table, and chair. A small window caught the sunlight. Into this room, Paton's father would retreat, sometimes three times a day, to study his Bible and pray. Often the children could hear his voice through the cracks in the wall.

Those memories never faded from Paton's soul, and years later he explained his own commitment to Christ by referring to his father, saying, "He walked with God; why may not I?"[3]

Our children see us watching television and reading the paper. They see us paying the bills and composing our shopping lists. But do they ever see us pouring over the Word of God? Do they ever hear us pray?

 Let's Talk: **Did your parents study their Bibles and pray openly in the home? What's keeping you from personal prayer and Bible reading?**

Habit 3: Empowered Parents Teach Their Children Diligently

"Love the Lord your God with all your heart and with all your soul and with all your strength. These commandments that I give you today are to be upon your hearts. Impress them on your children" (Deuteronomy 6:5-7).

This passage goes on to tell us how. We don't line up our kids as new recruits at boot camp and scream at them. We share the Scriptures naturally, spontaneously.

"Talk about them when you sit at home and when you walk along the road, when you lie down and when you get up" (Deuteronomy 6:7).

For example, one of the most important verses for all of us to learn is Proverbs 15:1: "A gentle answer turns away wrath." If children learn the principle of *underreaction* early in life, they'll have an advantage over others throughout their days.

But how do you teach them? You share it with them, and help them memorize it. You memorize it as a family, and talk about it. But it's in their everyday experience that those words come to life.

I attended graduate school at Wheaton College outside Chicago. One of the professors there, Dr. Robert Webber, tells a story from his childhood in Pennsylvania. The Webber's home backed up to a field belonging to the next farm, and blackberry bushes grew along the property lines. When he was about 9, Robert took a 10-gallon pail and filled it with blackberries. Suddenly, the neighboring farmer came out his house and started yelling, "Get out of my field!" he cried. "And don't let me catch you on my property ever again! Do you understand me?"

Robert ran to the house to tell his dad. "Give me that pail of blackberries," his father said. "We're going next door and talk to that man."

Robert thought to himself, *Good. My dad will show him a thing or two!*

"Mr. Farmer," Robert's dad said calmly, "I'm sorry my son was on your property." Then, handing the pail of blackberries to the farmer, he said, "Here, I want you to have these blackberries."

The farmer was taken aback. He waved his arm and said, "Hey, I'm sorry I yelled at the boy. I don't want the blackberries; I don't even like them. You keep them and pick all the berries you want."

As they walked home, Mr. Webber turned to his son and said, "The Scripture says, 'A gentle answer turns away wrath.' Remember that."

Robert Webber said, "I may not always have lived up to them, but I have never forgotten those words or my dad's action that gave those words meaning."[4]

What had happened? A young boy was melted and molded for good —and for God—by a dad who loved the Lord, who poured over the Bible, and who knew the Scriptures well enough to talk about them as they walked along the way.

 **Scripture Search:** Proverbs 14 and 15 are full of practical verses for daily home life. Read the verses I have selected below and circle the one that will most benefit you and your family right now if memorized and obeyed.

He who fears the Lord has a secure fortress,
 and for his children it will be a refuge (Proverbs 14:26).

A patient man has great understanding,
 but a quick-tempered man displays folly (Proverbs 14:29).

A gentle answer turns away wrath,
 but a harsh word stirs up anger (Proverbs 15:1).

Better a little with the fear of the Lord
 than great wealth with turmoil (Proverbs 15:16).

The fear of the Lord teaches a man wisdom,
 and humility comes before honor (Proverbs 15:33).

Why did you choose the particular verse you circled?

_____

The story of Adam and Eve, Cain and Abel—that first family—tells us that the problems in our homes are not primarily emotional, social, or psychological. They are primarily spiritual. Consequently, if we're going to be effective parents with confident kids, we need to build on a spiritual foundation. We have to know and love Jesus Christ. That's the only beginning there is.

P.S. (Practical Suggestions)

Habit 1 of empowered parents is to love the Lord deeply. Determine the depth of your love by completing the following spiritual inventory.

1. Choose a quiet hour or half hour for reflection. Find a place free from interruptions. If indoors, unhook the phone.

2. Begin by praying this prayer aloud: Dear God, You have demonstrated Your love for me by dying on the cross. You have told me that the greatest commandment for me is to love You with all my heart. Now search me, O God, and know my heart; test me and know my thoughts. See if there is any offensive way in me, and lead me in the way everlasting. Help me leave this time completely yielded to the Lord Jesus Christ. Amen.

3. Answer each of these questions.
   - What am I doing when I feel happiest?
   - What best satisfies my inner aches?
   - What or whom do I most fear losing?
   - What loss would cause me greatest distress?

   When you've answered these questions, you've discovered your god. Perhaps you'll find it's another person. Perhaps a goal or dream, a possession or hobby. Maybe a career or job.

4. Write a prayer of confession and dedication to the Lord. Read it out loud to Him. Begin choosing day-by-day to love Jesus above all else.

Habit 2 of empowered parents is studying the Word of God daily. Begin reading a chapter each day from the Scripture. Begin with the Gospels—Matthew, Mark, Luke, or John. Look for a verse to claim as your own. End your Bible reading with prayer for your children.

Habit 3 is sharing the Word of God with your children. As you uncover verses and promises from the Bible, look for opportunities to share them with your children. You may want to memorize some verses together as a family. Try some of the verses I have mentioned.

---

[1]For further information, read *Breaking the Cycle of Hurtful Family Experiences* (Nashville: LifeWay, 1994).

[2]"Start Young ... Give Small Doses," *Family Life Today,* ed. Fritz Ridenour, January 1975, 4.

[3]Julia H. Johnston, *Fifty Missionary Heroes Every Boy and Girl Should Know* (New York: Fleming H. Revell Company, 1913), 148-149.

[4]Robert Webber, "A Father's Influence," *What My Parents Did Right,* ed. Gloria Gaither (Nashville: Star Song Publishing Group, 1991), 207-208.

Home Turf

Stages of a Successful Marriage

Successful Single Parenting

Successful Blending and Stepparenting

❧ 2 ❧
Stages of a Successful Marriage

A man approached me at the end of a parenting seminar and said, "I came here thinking you were going to tell me how to become a better parent." He paused, and I thought he was going to complain. But he smiled and continued, "Instead you told me how to become a better person and a better husband."

Bingo.

It's our maturity as a person and our stability as a spouse that provides the emotional foundation for effective parenting.

I grew up on the back of bicycles, discarded bikes my dad found and fixed up for me. They were my best friends, and I flew all over town on them. I rode my bike to school in the winter, to the pool in the summer, and everywhere in between. One day I told my dad I'd like to learn to ride a unicycle. He used his welder on an old bike and converted it. I tried repeatedly to ride my new, single-axle vehicle, but I never succeeded. After a week's practice, I managed to remain balanced for only two seconds. I've seen some people do amazing things on unicycles, but one wheel proved difficult for me. I prefer two.

Children can likewise often travel further, easier with two wheels. God's optimum environment for a child is a loving, two-parent home. That's why the best thing a dad can do for his child is to cherish his wife. The best thing a wife can do for her kids is to adore her husband.

During the presidential race of 1992, Vice President Dan Quayle was ridiculed by the media for questioning the values of a popular television show in which a career woman chose to raise a child out of wedlock. But just four months after the election, the cover of *The Atlantic Monthly* blazed with these words: "Dan Quayle Was Right! After decades of public dispute about so-called family diversity, the evidence from social-science research is coming in: The dissolution of two-parent families, though it may benefit the adults involved, is harmful to many children, and dramatically undermines our society."[1]

The author, Barbara Dafoe Whitehead, asserts, "Research shows that many children from disrupted families have a harder time achieving intimacy in a relationship, forming a stable marriage, or even holding a steady job."[2]

Judith Wallerstein has accumulated research showing that children of divorce often suffer long into adulthood. Claire Berman has written the book *Adult Children of Divorce Speak Out.* "Berman tries to be unbiased about the outcome of divorce on grown-up kids. From anecdotes gleaned as president of the Stepfamily Association of America—and the latest social research—she recounts stories of adult children who do become more empathetic, independent, committed to marriage.

"But her heart is revealed: 'Divorce is not good for children ... There is just no getting around it.' She develops the traumas: problems trusting others; becoming intimate; achieving self-esteem; and the needs for control, success and money. And children of divorce are more apt to divorce."[3]

The Old Testament's Last Word on Parenting

The Bible was right all along. The millions of dollars invested in thousands of studies over the last 20 years only confirm what the Bible said 2,400 years ago:

> *Another thing you do: You flood the Lord's altar with tears. You weep and wail because he no longer pays attention to your offerings or accepts them with pleasure from your hands. You ask, "Why?" It is because the Lord is acting as the witness between you and the wife of your youth, because you have broken faith with her, though she is your partner, the wife of your marriage covenant (Malachi 2:13-14).*

Malachi, the last of the Old Testament prophets, warned the people that, though they didn't realize it, they were drifting from the Lord. "He isn't accepting your offerings or your gifts," Malachi cried, "because you have a terrible problem in your homes." The men were not remaining true to their marriage vows. They were cheating on their wives, violating their marriage covenant. They were breaking faith with their spouses, though God intended to make them one. "Has not the Lord made them one?" continued Malachi (Malachi 2:15).

When a man and woman exchange wedding vows, they have the freedom and pleasure to become physically, intimately, sexually one. They become one body. They gradually become one in the purpose of their lives and in the attitudes of their hearts.

Why? Read on: "And why one? Because he was seeking godly offspring" (Malachi 2:15).

"It was so you would have children, and then lead them to become God's people" (Malachi 2:15, CEV). Of all the systems for child rearing God could have designed, a happy, holy marriage provides the optimum environment for raising kids in the nurture and instruction of the Lord. God could have sent angels to earth, staffing heaven-run nurseries. He could have placed them in boarding schools beyond the stars. God could have devised a million different ways for children. But the best way in all the universe is a home in which a man and a woman are one in flesh and spirit. "So," Malachi continued,

> *... guard yourself in your spirit, and do not break faith with the wife of your youth. "I hate divorce," says the Lord God of Israel, "and I hate a man's covering himself with violence as well as with his garment," says the Lord Almighty. So guard yourselves in your spirit, and do not break faith (Malachi 2:15-16).*

Guard ourselves? Guard our homes? How do we do that? We must realize that most marriages move through five stages.

The Five Stages of Marriage
Dream Stage

When a man and a woman meet, date, drool, and fall in love, it's with the lilt and lightness of a lovely dream. Candlelight flickers. In the passion of the moment, they engage and marry. It's a dream come true. This is the stage pictured in the bridal magazines, with their advertisements showing couples cavorting in heart-shaped bathtubs in the Pocono Mountains or strolling hand-in-hand on tropical beaches. Cupid's arrow finds its mark.

This stage usually lasts two days into the honeymoon.

Sometimes only two hours.

Demanding Stage

Marriage brings swift, unexpected challenges, and love quickly enters a demanding stage. We gradually realize that our spouse has more flaws than we thought. Our spouse places more demands on us than we want to fulfill. Couples typically enter their honeymoon immature and inexperienced. They begin to feel tension they hadn't anticipated. The wife expects the husband to make certain contributions to the relationship, and the husband expects the wife to conform to his self-styled criteria.

My wife was disappointed with me early in our marriage. She had expected me to be her handsome prince, opening doors for her, taking out the trash, making the bed when I slept late, volunteering to do household chores, considering her wishes when we sat down to watch television, and offering to spend my Saturdays doing what she wanted.

I didn't realize she harbored those expectations, and I probably would have resented them anyway. I'd been living on my own for too long, molding my life around my pursuits and style. I had my own way of doing things, my own hobbies, my own interests. I had controlled my checkbook and credit cards for a long time, and it had been years since anyone had told me what I should or shouldn't watch on television. I wasn't used to someone controlling my time. And why should anyone care if I left the medicine chest open, the commode lid up, and the towels hung from the doorknob? It was none of her business.

But it was even worse.

I not only didn't want to conform to her expectations, I selfishly thought she should conform to mine. I wanted someone to run three miles with me for exercise; cook like a gourmet chef; keep house like a British maid; bring in a sizable income; meet my physical needs whenever I desired; adopt my taste in clothes, entertainment, and lifestyle; treat my family as though they were her own; can produce from the garden like my mother; entertain all my buddies who dropped in to visit; and leave my checkbook alone.

The dream faded and Katrina's disappointment grew—a condition experienced by most newly-married couples. Looking back, she now admits that adjusting to married life after years of being single was one of the most difficult adjustments she's ever had to make. Ditto for me.

24

Drudgery Stage

As couples encounter the frustrations and disappointments of marriage, they begin to enter the drudgery stage. They typically plod on, trying to salvage the dream, but it increasingly becomes a bad dream, sometimes a nightmare. The man grows angry and distant; the woman, disappointed and disillusioned. Sometimes, couples become bogged down at this stage; it can go on a long time.

I recently counseled a couple whose marriage is mired in this kind of mud. The husband works long days, comes home, and flops in front of the television where he dozes for a half hour before grabbing a sandwich and heading to the bowling lanes. His wife, who also puts in a stressful day's work, returns home at roughly the same time, but she retires to the bedroom and talks to friends on the phone. Both seem angry and minimal communication is occurring between them. The husband recently said, "We just don't have anything in common. She doesn't like sports, and I don't like her circle of friends. We go out sometimes, but we usually end up fighting. I guess we've just decided we prefer no communication to bad communication; so we just don't talk to each other very often."

Decision Stage

Sooner or later, it will lead to the decision stage. Love is, after all, nothing less nor more than a choice. Love isn't so much a matter of candlelight, but commitment. The Bible offers many passages about marriage, but we usually don't think of Colossians 3:23-24 as one of them. We should, for its application to matrimony is profound.

> *Work hard and cheerfully at all you do, just as though you were working for the Lord and not merely for your masters, remembering that it is the Lord Christ who is going to pay you, giving you your full portion of all he owns (Colossians 3:23-24, TLB).*

Successful couples are the ones who decide to work hard and cheerfully on their marriages.

Years ago I spent a day in a Chicago divorce court, doing research for a school assignment. I was the only observer who occupied a seat in the courtroom for the whole day; and at the end of it, the bailiff told me the judge wanted to see me in his chambers.

"Son, I've seen you all day in my courtroom," he said.

"Yes, sir. I'm researching a paper about family relationships."

"Well," he said, leaning back and looking like a wise old owl, "let me tell you something, and don't ever forget it. I've been sitting on this bench many years, and I've presided over the funerals of thousands of marriages. They all had one thing in common. The couples forgot to work on their marriages.

"Young man," he continued, "marriage takes work. You have to work on it every day. Don't ever forget that."

He's right.

Alan McGinnis, in his book, *The Power of Optimism,* points out:

A marriage will not continue to be good simply because two people love each other, are compatible, and get off to a fine start. To the contrary, marriages left to their own devices tend to wear out, break down, and ultimately disintegrate.[4]

Author Robert Anderson says, "In every marriage more than a week old, there are grounds for divorce. The trick is to find, and continue to find, grounds for marriage."[5]

Scripture Search: **The marriage of Aquila and Priscilla seems to have been one of the best partnerships in Scripture. While we don't have extensive biblical data about it, there is enough for us to read between the lines. As you read the following passages, write in the margin any characteristics or clues that help explain their positive relationship.**

After this, Paul left Athens and went to Corinth. There he met a Jew named Aquila, a native of Pontus, who had recently come from Italy with his wife Priscilla, because Claudius had ordered all the Jews to leave Rome. Paul went to see them, and because he was a tentmaker as they were, he stayed and worked with them (Acts 18:1-3).

Paul stayed on in Corinth for some time. Then he left the brothers and sailed for Syria, accompanied by Priscilla and Aquila. ... They arrived in Ephesus, where Paul left Priscilla and Aquila (Acts 18:18-19).

Meanwhile a Jew named Apollos, a native of Alexandria, came to Ephesus. He was a learned man, with a thorough knowledge of the Scriptures. He had been instructed in the way of the Lord, and he spoke with great fervor and taught about Jesus accurately, though he knew only the baptism of John. He began to speak boldly in the synagogue. When Priscilla and Aquila heard him, they invited him to their home and explained to him the way of God more adequately (Acts 18:24-26).

Greet Priscilla and Aquila, my fellow workers in Christ Jesus. They risked their lives for me. Not only I but all the churches of the Gentiles are grateful to them. Greet also the church that meets at their house (Romans 16:3-4).

What one way would you like your marriage to be more like Priscilla and Aquila's?

_____

Delight Stage

If you and your spouse will work on your marriage, it'll enter the delight stage. The husband in the Song of Songs told his bride, "How delightful is your love" (Song of Songs 4:10). While all around us marriages grow cheaper, ours can grow deeper. We encounter a few storms, but no shipwreck. We have a few scars, but many stars; and through it we'll find we have groaned a little but grown a lot.

 Let's Talk: **Can you identify any of these stages in your marriage? What stage are you presently in? What actions may be necessary to move on to the next stage? How might your parenting skills be affected by the stage your marriage is in right now?**

ABCs of a Mature Marriage

I have found the following ABCs to be effective in developing a mature marriage.

A = Adequate rest. Many marriages falter and fail because the two partners are so exhausted they don't have the necessary energy to work on their relationship. In many homes, both partners are trying to hold down jobs—sometimes multiple jobs. With the demands of home, church, job, hobbies, civic clubs, schools, child rearing, community, and extended family, there isn't time for necessary leisure. Americans are working over 150 more hours a year than they did two decades ago. That's the equivalent of an extra month per year, and the hardest hit group is 18- to 39-year-old working mothers. One of them said, "I work like a dog. When I come home, I'm tired. I find myself short-tempered because there's so much to do and no way to get it all done."[6]

Tired people don't handle emotions well. I have a daughter who used to alarm us by bursting into tears over all sorts of things, sometimes big things and sometimes small. We couldn't pull her out of her hysteria. But we finally noticed this only happened when she was exhausted. We learned the only remedy was to get her to bed and let her sleep. She was fine in the morning.

We're all like that to an extent, and one of the reasons our homes become emotionally distraught is that we're exhausted. A new book entitled *The Twenty-Four-Hour Society* demonstrates that fatigue has been at the bottom of many of the headline-grabbing disasters of our day, such as the Bhopal disaster, the *Exxon Valdez* oil spill, the Three Mile Island nuclear accident, the Chernobyl disaster, and the shooting down of an Iranian jet by the *USS Vincennes.* NASA officials made the ill-fated decision to launch the Space Shuttle *Challenger* after working 20 hours straight with only two to three hours sleep the night before.[7]

Fatigue is at the root of many family explosions, too. Wise couples cut out superfluous activities in order to get the rest they need.

Scripture Search: Read Psalm 127 below.

If the Lord does not build the house,
    the work of the builders is useless;
if the Lord does not protect the city,
    it does no good for sentries to stand guard.
It is useless to work so hard for a living,
    getting up early and going to bed late.
For the Lord provides for those he loves,
    while they are asleep.

Children are a gift from the Lord;
    they are a real blessing.
The sons a man has when he is young
    are like arrows in a soldier's hand.
Happy is the man who has many such arrows.
He will never be defeated
    when he meets his enemies in the place of judgment
(Psalm 127, GNB).

The first part of the Psalm tells us (✓check one):
❑ God wants us to work ourselves to death.
❑ We don't need to work or labor, for God does everything on our behalf.
❑ Burning the candle on both ends is wise.
❑ God doesn't want us to live in perpetual exhaustion, for He knows we need adequate sleep.
❑ We don't need home security devices, for God will protect our residences.

How does the emphasis of the first half of Psalm 127 (God grants us rest rather than chronic exhaustion) relate to the last half of the Psalm (God wants to bless us as parents)?

_____

_____

B = Be gentle. Most people today have damaged egos. They're struggling to hang on to the shreds of their self-esteem. When you and your mate constantly argue, and you emotionally attack each other, and you're cutting and harsh and sarcastic … you'll destroy your home. The Bible says, "Be completely humble and gentle; be patient, bearing with one another in love" (Ephesians 4:2).

Let's Talk: **What's the difference between being gentle and being passive or weak? What are some qualities of gentleness? How can a person begin to acquire gentleness?**

Scripture Search: **Galatians 5:22-23 lists nine different attitudes. On a scale from 1 (low) to 10 (high), rate yourself as a spouse and as a parent in each of these areas. Don't take time for in-depth thought; write the number that first comes to mind.**

	As a spouse	As a parent
Love	_____	_____
Joy	_____	_____
Peace	_____	_____
Patience	_____	_____
Kindness	_____	_____
Goodness	_____	_____
Faithfulness	_____	_____
Gentleness	_____	_____
Self-control	_____	_____

Notice the number you put beside *gentleness*. ✓ Check the box by the correct word to complete the following verses.

A gentle answer turns away … ❑ wrath ❑ peace,
but a harsh word stirs up anger (Proverbs 15:1).

Through patience a ruler can be persuaded,
and a gentle … ❑ arm ❑ tongue … can break the bone
(Proverbs 25:15).

"Take my yoke upon you and … ❑ hear ❑ learn … from me,
for I am gentle and humble in heart, and you will find …
❑ rest   ❑ trouble … for your souls" (Matthew 11:29).

Brothers, if someone is caught in a sin, you who are ... ❑ nosy ❑ spiritual ... should restore him gently (Galatians 6:1).

Be completely humble and gentle; be ... ❑ patient ❑ persistent, ... bearing with one another in love (Ephesians 4:2).

Rejoice in the Lord always. I will say it again: Rejoice! Let your ... ❑ gentleness ❑ pride ... be evident to all. The Lord is near (Philippians 4:4-5).

Circle the verse above that needs to be posted on the "refrigerator door" of your mind. Why did you choose that one?

_____

*C = **Compromise**.* When a statesman goes overseas to mediate a peace accord between two hostile nations, his major effort is to bring both parties into zones of compromise. That's also among the primary jobs of marriage counselors. Not even identical twins share the same views on everything. We're all different, coming from various backgrounds, displaying unique personalities, temperaments, and opinions. Compromise is a critical skill in building a partnership.

My wife and I are very different. She's from New England, and I'm from Tennessee. She's Scandinavian, and I'm southern. I come from an affectionate family, but my wife is Finnish, and the Finns are not generally known as affectionate people.

We have different family traditions, different tastes in food and leisure, even different views about biblical doctrine. We've had to learn to appreciate each other's distinctiveness and to compromise on areas that could have grown bitter.

*D = **Date**.* Doug Fields, a marriage therapist from California, warns that many couples, once they are married, assume they can no longer date or romance each other. "I'm convinced," he writes "that the lack of dating and romance in marriage is one of the major causes of a broken relationship."[8]

My wife and I have to work hard to carve out dates, largely due to a busy career and the demands of three highly-involved children. We've found we can easily manage breakfast together at a nearby restaurant on Monday mornings, and we use this time to review our calendars and coordinate our schedules. About once a month we opt for an evening out on the town, though sometimes we have to improvise. One month, for example, when the kids were all supposed to be gone for the evening, we decided to go out to eat, then come home early to relax. But as it turned out, our home was unexpectedly taken over by teenagers whose plans had changed, one of whom (our daughter) also commandeered our pocket money. Our plans were shot.

We went out anyway to a cheap but friendly restaurant, then returned to my office where we pulled in some overstuffed chairs from the conference room, rolled in a VCR from the audio-visual storage room, popped some corn in the office microwave, and watched a movie we'd wanted to see for a long time.

We enjoyed it thoroughly.

We've actually learned that a *date* can be something as simple as a cup of coffee alone in the dining room after the girls have fled the supper table. But however you do it, it's essential to spend relaxed time together building your relationship.

Let's Talk: **When was the last time you and your spouse had a date like the ones you had before you tied the knot? What are some of your favorite mate-date activities?**

E = Every day spend time with the Lord. Katrina and I, despite an unpromising beginning, have been blessed through the years with a happy marriage, and for that I give credit to one man—James (Buck) Hatch, professor at Columbia Bible College. His psychology course on marriage and family life showed us how to have a happy home. And he lives what he teaches. He and his wife, Mittie, have enjoyed 51 years of marriage, raising four sons in the process who all entered various areas of Christian service.

His secret?

From the start, Buck and Mittie committed themselves to maintaining a growing relationship with God, a relationship their sons witnessed. "Both Mom and Dad were absolutely consistent in their spiritual disciplines," they report. "Early in the morning, Dad would be in the living room and Mom in the bedroom—work day or vacation—with the Scripture and in prayer."[9]

The daily commitment to walk with God carried them through the inevitable conflicts brought on by human selfishness. A mature marriage requires spiritually mature people, and that comes from spending time every day with the Lord.

If you and your spouse will work on your marriage with the Lord, no matter what stage you are in, you will model a godly marriage for your children and provide them a framework for security and confidence. You'll establish the environment necessary for raising your children in the nurture and instruction of the Lord.

You will have started empowered parenting.

P.S. (Practical Suggestions from Chapter 2)

1. Plan a date with your spouse. Arrange a meal in a nice restaurant, and during dinner:

- Talk about which of the five stages your marriage is in.
- Ask each other, "What one thing can we do that would most improve our marriage?"
- Discuss your schedules, and find one thing you're doing that you can eliminate to have more time for rest, leisure, and family.

2. Memorize Ephesians 4:2 (see page 29). You may want to post this verse on the refrigerator or on the bathroom mirror until it has been assimilated into your heart.

3. Sit down with your spouse and a calendar. Pencil in several evenings during the coming months when you can take one another on dates.

4. Begin the habit of morning devotions. If not at daybreak, set aside at least 10 minutes during the day for Bible reading and prayer.

[1] "Dan Quayle Was Right," *The Atlantic Monthly,* April 1993, cover.
[2] Barbara Dafoe Whitehead, "Dan Quayle Was Right," *The Atlantic Monthly,* April 1993, 47.
[3] Karen S. Peterson, "Children of Divorce: No Age Limit to Hurt," *USA Today,* 11 April 1991, 4D.
[4] Alan Loy McGinnis, *The Power of Optimism* (San Francisco: Harper & Row, 1990), 45.
[5] Ibid., 113.
[6] Tammy Joyner and Noreen Seebacher, "Is There Life Out There?" *The Tennessean,* March 8, 1993, E1.
[7] Martin Moore-Ede, *The Twenty-Four-Hour Society* (New York: Addison-Wesley, 1993), 3-7.
[8] Doug Fields, "Date Your Mate," *Focus on the Family,* February 1992, 3.
[9] Camille Burner, "Above All Else," *Moody,* February 1993, 25.

❧ 3 ❧
Successful Single Parenting

Being a single parent isn't easy. If you don't believe me, just ask a single parent what life is like, that is, if you can pin one down for a few minutes. You can always spot a single parent at a school function. They're the ones who look proud, tired, and rushed and maybe a little distant. That's because they are busily calculating the rest of the day. Their minds are racing: *Now let's see, if Johnny's group performs in the next 15 minutes, then I can dash across town and if I don't hit any red lights, I can get there in time to see Susy play soccer, and if I just stay long enough to see one quarter, I can get back here to pick up Johnny before the end of his performance. Then I can rush back, get Susy, go home, make dinner, do the laundry, help with homework, get the kids to bed, put the clothes in the dryer, get my clothes ready for work in the morning. Maybe I'll get to bed by midnight. Oh well, that's earlier than last night.* And the mind just keeps clicking away.

It was never God's design for children to be parented by only one person. God's optimum environment for child rearing is a two-parent Christian home where both parents love each other and are forging a strong marriage. But, we don't live in an ideal world or always enjoy optimum environments. Statistics tell us that one-parent homes are rapidly increasing in America today. Some experts are predicting that 50 to 60 percent of all children born today will live in single-parent homes for some period of their lives. The 1990 census of my own city of Nashville showed that 35 percent of all households with children in my county are headed by single parents.[1]

The Struggles of Single Parents

It isn't easy. Single parents know how challenging it can be raising children alone. But many in traditional two-parent homes don't sufficiently understand those challenges and need to consider some of the pressures bearing on single parents. That's why all of us should read this chapter. Church leaders should consider the needs of this growing constituency with understanding, support, and grace. That's why reading this chapter is important for all of them.

 Let's Talk: **Did you grow up in a single-parent home during part or all of your childhood? What were the advantages? The disadvantages? Are you currently a single parent? What are the pluses and minuses of being a single parent?**

Consider seven struggles that many single parents silently endure. The first involves finding **adequate adult role models** for their children. Studies have shown that very few kids from divorced homes have mentors—older adults who exercise a positive moral and emotional influence. Male role models for boys are a particular concern. I've had single mothers tell me, "I just wish there was some man in our church who would take my boy under his wing." Many mothers harbor a secret fear that their boys will grow up with homosexual tendencies if they don't have positive, masculine father-figures with whom to bond in their early years.

Another challenge is **financial**. Ninety percent of all single-parent homes are headed by mothers, and ninety percent of all single mothers in America make less than $15,000 a year. Statistically, the level of income for women decreases 76 percent after a divorce. Just imagine if your family income was suddenly cut by 76 percent. Furthermore, child support often isn't paid as it should be.[2]

Adequate time is also a struggle. Single parents have to be father, mother, wage earner, maintenance person, mechanic, housekeeper, cook, yard worker, nurse, counselor, occasional veterinarian, chauffeur, money manager, window washer, laundry person, tutor, "read to me-er," and worship leader—with no one to relieve the pressures.

One single mother said, "The hardest thing about being a single parent is that there's no one in the bullpen." It's like playing the whole ball game without any relief.

A fourth struggle is **loneliness.** Florence Cherry of Cornell University said, "When I ask people in my groups what's the hardest thing about being a single working parent, they invariably say that when you're married and you roll over in bed at night after a long, hard day, you rub against a warm body; but when you're single and roll over in bed at night after a long, hard day, you run the risk of falling out."[3]

Karen Levine said in *Parents*, "The issue of loneliness is universal for single parents—whether they are divorced, widowed, or have never been married."[4]

For many single parents, there's no one immediately accessible to share burdens with, no one to talk to, no one to lean on.

A fifth struggle is **perception**. A lot of single parents feel the rest of the world views them as second-class citizens and second-class parents. This perception needs to change.

A sixth struggle concerns **lack of available child care**. When I need to be out in the evening, I know Katrina can be at home with the kids. When she needs to be out, I can be home. But a single parent does not have that kind of support. The trouble and expense of arranging what often seems like an endless supply of child care is harrowing.

And a final struggle, especially for single custodial mothers, is the **sense of competition with the children's father**. Mom often sees Dad having all the fun with the children while she shoulders the day-to-day responsibilities. What's more, she notices that the kids are more excited about visits with Dad than they are about returning home. Emotionally, that can be very painful.

What can be done? Let's look at this from three perspectives: what single parents can do, what the church can do, and what God can do.

What Single Parents Can Do

What are some empowered-parenting strategies for single parents?

First, recognize **you are a family**. Sandra Aldrich recalls when her daughter Holly "was in the third grade she came home one day in tears. One of the room mothers had handed out printed directions to a special event and said, 'Take these home to your families.' Then she glanced at Holly and said, 'Sorry. I mean "to your *moms.*" ' " Holly's dad had died four months before. In the kitchen, Sandra Aldrich put her arms around Holly and said, " 'Holly, we are still a family. We're just a family of *three* now.' " That moment changed both of them.[5]

Second, **lean on your extended family and friends**. In biblical times, people depended heavily on their relatives and friends; they helped one another. When Joseph and Mary took 12-year-old Jesus to Jerusalem, they didn't realize He had not turned homeward with them, and that for three days He was alone in the biggest and most frightening metropolitan area of their country. It sounds like a plot for another *Home Alone* movie. But Joseph and Mary hadn't been irresponsible; they assumed Jesus was in the care of an extended family member. In biblical times, both parents worked. The husband and wife worked in the fields; the wife also worked in the village, in the marketplace, and in the home. Just read the range of responsibilities borne by the godly woman described in Proverbs 31.

They depended on their extended family and friends to help them with their children. Even today in our more mobile society, I know of many cases where grandparents, uncles and aunts, and friends have taken children under their wings and helped a parent with their load.

My dad was raised by a single mother, for his dad died when he was seven. Being the youngest of seven children, he had the benefit of older siblings. The oldest child, in fact, became like a father to my dad.

It's all right to lean on others; it's all right to ask for help.

Third, **don't expect your children to provide for your emotional needs** as your spouse would have. It's important to have loving interdependence with one another—a close parent-child bond. But your children are going to grow up and leave home. If you become overly dependent upon them, it can become a dysfunctional situation.

We all need to love and receive love in healthy ways, but single parents shouldn't depend on their children to meet their emotional needs.

 Let's Talk: **If single parents shouldn't totally draw emotional support from their children, where do they fill their emotional tanks?**

Fourth, **single parents must take time for themselves**, every day. John Rosenmond, author and family psychologist, wrote "After divorce, many single parents try too hard to compensate for the absence of a spouse. In the process, they neglect their own needs in order to meet their children's needs. These well-meaning single moms and dads often fail to understand that they can't take good care of their kids without first taking good care of themselves."[6]

This is biblical. When Paul spoke to the church leaders in Ephesus, he told them (note the order): "Keep watch *over yourselves* and all the flock of which the Holy Spirit has made you overseers" (Acts 20:28).

A hot bath, an evening out, a cup of hot chocolate, a weekend get-away, an hour's Bible study, an engaging hobby. Think of yourself as your own best friend, and take care of yourself for the sake of your children—the flock over which the Holy Spirit has made you overseer.

But fifth and most importantly, **single parents need to walk closely with God.** Pray, study God's word, and trust Him.

Scripture Search: Read the verses below.

"Submit yourselves, then, to God. Resist the devil, and he will flee from you. Come near to God and he will come near to you" (James 4:7-8).

"Let us draw near to God with a sincere heart in full assurance of faith" (Hebrews 10:22).

What do these verses say we must do to draw near to God?
✓ Check all that apply.
❏ Call out God's name.
❏ Approach God with a sincere heart.
❏ Resist the devil.
❏ Come before God with singing.
❏ Submit to God.
❏ Come to God in faith and He will come to us.

If we approach God with a sincere heart and in faith, resisting the temptations of the devil and submitting to God's will, He will draw near to us.

What the Church Can Do

Christians must be sensitive to the needs of single parents and their children. Could you provide emotional support and encouragement, or make room in your life for a fatherless or motherless boy or girl?

Recently at a church-related social function, I sat by a 13-year old boy whose parents are divorced. He lives with his mother, and he's active in our church's youth group. I leaned over to him and asked, "James, how's school?"

"Not very good."

"What's wrong? Don't you like it?"

"Oh, I like it all right, but I'm not making the grades."

"Don't understand the material?" I probed. "Need some tutoring?"

"I understand the material. I just don't do my homework."

"Why?"

"I just don't. It takes too long. I'd be up all night."

I'm not above bribery, so I said to him, "Let's make a deal. If you do all your homework this week and tell me about it next Sunday, we'll go out for a banana split together. OK?"

"OK," he said with a grin.

He kept his end of the bargain, I kept mine, and we've been periodically reviewing his progress ever since.

All he needed was a little attention.

I've found that children from single-parent homes are very affectionate. A word, a hug, a trip to the ice cream shop, a little attention—those things pay higher than average dividends.

All of us can do some of those "little" things in the name of Christ.

Larger endeavors can be undertaken together with other Christians. Almost any church, even the smallest, can launch vital programs aimed at single-parent needs.

For example, why not have a group of holy handymen (and handy women) that single mothers could call for help with leaky faucets and broken window panes? Why couldn't a group of mechanically-minded men and women help single mothers with minor car repairs and oil changes? It wouldn't be hard to develop this kind of ministry, and what a world of good they would do!

Even the youth group can become involved. Teenagers excel at mowing lawns and taking care of younger children.

Churches need to develop a budget and programs for single parents. Sunday school classes, weeknight socials, weekly support groups, divorce recovery groups, weekend get-aways and retreats, exercise classes with child care provided—all those things are vital for growing churches wanting to reach single parents.

And speaking of child care, church leaders can no longer assume that homes have built-in baby sitters. Single parents face difficulty attending church activities unless child care is provided

 Let's Talk: **Are you or your church doing anything to support and encourage single parents? What simple steps would improve your ministry in this area?**

 Scripture Search: **Read the following verses from Psalm 103. Circle words or phrases in the text that describe God's model for us as we understand and encourage single parents.**

The Lord is compassionate and gracious,
    slow to anger, abounding in love.

He will not always accuse,
    nor will he harbor his anger forever;
he does not treat us as our sins deserve
    or repay us according to our iniquities.
For as high as the heavens are above the earth,
    so great is his love for those who fear him;
as far as the east from the west,
    so far has he removed our transgressions from us.
As a father has compassion on his children,
    so the Lord has compassion on those who fear him.
From everlasting to everlasting
    the Lord's love is with those who fear him,
    and his righteousness with their children's children—
with those who keep his covenant
    and remember to obey his precepts.
The Lord has established his throne in heaven,
    and his kingdom rules over all …
Praise the Lord O my soul (Psalm 103:8-13,17-19,22).

What God Can Do

Perhaps the best biblical passage about single parents is in Genesis 21.

> *Early the next morning Abraham took some food and a skin of water and gave them to Hagar. He set them on her shoulders and then sent her off with the boy. She went on her way and wandered in the desert of Beersheba. When the water in the skin was gone, she put the boy under one of the bushes. Then she went off and sat down nearby, about a bowshot away, for she thought, "I cannot watch the boy die." As she sat there nearby, she began to sob.*
>
> *God heard the boy crying, and the angel of God called to Hagar from heaven and said to her, "What is the matter, Hagar? Do not be afraid; God has heard the boy crying as he lies there. Lift the boy up and take him by the hand, for I will make him into a great nation."*
>
> *Then God opened her eyes and she saw a well of water. So she went and filled the skin with water and gave the boy a drink. God was with the boy as he grew up (Genesis 21:14-20).*

Hagar was a single mother, cast out of Abraham's neighborhood, literally abandoned in the desert with only a skin of water. She came to the end of herself, and she put her son Ishmael under some bushes and left him, because she couldn't bear to watch him die. But God heard the boy crying and told her not to be afraid. God was watching over the two of them and promised to provide for them.

And God did.

Have you ever considered how many people in the Bible were raised in single-parent situations? Naomi and her husband settled in a foreign country, and when he died, she was left to raise her two sons alone. They both grew up to marry wonderful wives, and when the two sons died, Naomi cared for her daughter-in-law Ruth. She became Ruth's mentor and provider. Ruth, in turn, was an ancestor of Jesus.

Moses was scuttled from his parents' home by Pharaoh's decree. His parents placed him in a basket and set him adrift on the River Nile. The daughter of Pharaoh found him, loved him, and raised him by herself. He grew up to deliver the children of Israel from the Egyptians.

The widow of Zarephath in 1 Kings 17 was a single mother, reduced to starvation by a terrible drought. But God, seeing her plight, honored her faith. Through Elijah, God satisfied her needs.

When the widow in 2 Kings 4 was trying to raise her sons, the creditors came to take them into slavery to satisfy the family debt. But God intervened miraculously through the prophet Elisha.

Josiah, one of the greatest kings of the Old Testament, was raised by his mother after her husband was assassinated. Josiah was only eight years old when he lost his father to violence. But in that single-parent home he grew up to become one of Judah's greatest kings and a man who ignited revival in his land (see 2 Kings 22-23).

Queen Esther was raised by her older cousin Mordecai, a man of steel nerves and steady faith. When the Jews were facing apocalyptic danger, Esther, spurred by Mordecai, approached King Xerxes. She could have been killed for her boldness, but she said, " 'If I perish, I perish' " (Esther 4:16). Her intervention saved the Jewish race, and her exploits are honored each year at the Jewish feast of Purim.

The story of the widow of Nain in Luke 7 is an example of the grace and love of Jesus Christ for single parents. This woman had done her best in raising her son. But she couldn't raise him from the dead, and his final illness had left her bereaved and totally alone. Jesus came upon the funeral procession, stopped the bearers of the coffin, touched the boy, and raised him to life.

Jesus and His half-siblings were raised by a single mother after the death of her husband. We aren't sure when Joseph died, but he likely left behind a family with children still at home.

I believe Timothy is one of Scripture's prime examples of the power and provision of God in a single-parent home. Strictly speaking, Timothy's home may not have been single-parented. But his father was absent. God sent Paul to be like a father to the young Timothy and to mentor him. Late in life Paul wrote an affectionate letter to his young disciple, saying, "I have been reminded of your sincere faith, which first lived in your grandmother Lois and in your mother Eunice and now lives in you" (2 Timothy 1:5). "From childhood, you have known the Holy Scriptures that are able to make you wise for salvation through faith in Christ Jesus" (2 Timothy 3:15).

The evidence in the Bible is persuasive.

Children in single-parent homes can grow up to be strong, healthy, mature, and devout when raised in a home where Jesus Christ is present. The Lord is a Father to the fatherless; a Mother to the motherless;

a Husband to the widow; a Companion to the single parent.

Wherever God is worshiped, His grace is sufficient.

Whether a single parent or a husband or wife in a two-parent home, we parents can model a faith for our children patterned after that of Lois and Eunice. We can teach our children from infancy the holy Scriptures that are able to make them wise unto salvation through faith in Jesus Christ. We can train them in the way they should go and raise them in the nurture and instruction of the Lord. We can pray.

And the Lord will hear our cry. God still sends springs in the desert and streams in the valleys, as He did for Hagar. God loves all parents and their kids, whatever their situation.

That's why there's hope for all parents. And for their children!

P.S. (Practical Suggestions from Chapter 3)

1. If you are a single parent ...
   - Take time for yourself. Find a hobby or a pleasant activity to provide relaxation and leisure. Do something for yourself every day.
   - Study the single parents in the Bible, including the ones mentioned in this chapter. Ask God to teach you His ways through them.
   - Dedicate your children to the Lord. Claim God's wisdom, help, and oversight. Trust God with problems that only He can solve.
   - Find a strong single-parents' support group or Bible study. Begin making friends with others facing some of the same stresses you're facing. Add another single parent to your prayer list.

2. If you know a single parent ...
   - Add her or him to your prayer list. If you keep a prayer journal, devote a page to that parent. Ask about specific needs, list those in your journal, and let him or her know you're praying for them.
   - Adopt a single parent's kids. Schedule monthly outings; be a buddy; call about homework; remember them on birthdays and holidays.
   - Encourage your church to mobilize teams of men and women who are good at carpentry, electricity, plumbing, auto mechanics, small-engine repair, and lawn care. Offer this ministry to single parents.
   - Encourage your church to develop a scholarship fund for single parents' children to help defray the costs of church-related events.

---

[1]Information distributed by US Department of Commerce, Bureau of the Census, Document report on Davidson County, Tennessee, 148.

[2]Jerry Jones, ed., *Growing Your Single Adult Ministry* (Colorado Springs: David C. Cook, 1993), 285.

[3]Karen Levine, "Single ... With Children," *Parents,* December 1990, 73.

[4]Ibid., 73-74.

[5]Sandra Picklesimer Aldrich, "Secret Courage for Single Mothers," *Focus on the Family,* February 1992, 12.

[6]John Rosemond, "Raising A Child Alone," *Better Homes and Gardens,* April 1992, 33.

❦ 4 ❦
Successful Blending and Stepparenting

A young man sporting a positive attitude once told me that he was the luckiest person in the world because most people have only two parents, but I have four. He was more fortunate than he realized, for all four parents—his biological ones and their new spouses—had agreed to cooperate with one another in a parenting coalition aimed at providing him a positive environment. As a result, he felt doubly blessed.

"I love having a blended family," one mother said with exuberance. "I grew up in a large family, and I like having 6 kids. Being a school teacher, I put up with 30 children every day of the week. So for me, coming home to 6 is a breeze."

"Stepfathering has given me an unexpectedly close relationship with my wife's son," said Steve. "While he respects my authority in the family, he doesn't think of me as his father, but more like a big brother. We are pals, and our friendship has bonded in a kind of lateral way that wouldn't have been possible if I'd been his biological dad."

"Tom probably saved my life," admitted a young father, looking back on his teen years. "When my mom and dad divorced, I started getting pretty wild. Mom couldn't control me, and I think that's one reason she married Tom. She knew I needed more than she could give. Tom stepped in and talked with me and set some rules that I needed. I don't know what would have happened if he hadn't come along."

Are these comments the exceptions?

Stepfamilies, says psychologist Harold Bloomfield, are "born of loss,"[1] and at least by reputation leave a lot to be desired. Consider, for example, the evil stepmothers in Hansel and Gretel, Snow White, and Cinderella or the stepfamily horrors described in Dickens' novels.

If these negative images are accurate, we're a nation in trouble, for stepfamilies are rapidly becoming the predominant family form in America. One out of every three Americans is now a stepparent, stepchild, stepsibling, or some other member of a stepfamily. Over half of all Americans have been or will be in a blended family sometime during their lives. By the year 2000, more children will live in stepfamilies than in traditional homes.[2]

Yes, marriage should last a lifetime, divorce is never God's ideal, and children are hurt through the breakup of a home. In most cases, stepfamilies and blended families represent Plan B. But while differences of opinion exist among Christians as to the Scriptural teachings regarding divorce and remarriage, virtually all Christians agree that God's overwhelming grace extends to stepfamilies and blended families. He starts where we are, offering mercy, healing, and love.

41

Most stepfamilies aren't as bad as Cinderella's, but they do have more complicated problems than the traditional family. One of history's first blended families demonstrated the difficulties. The patriarch, Jacob, found himself in the unenviable position of having 12 sons and a daughter by 4 different women all at each other's throats and living under one roof. It took 30 years and a global famine to unite them.

Most blended families aren't composed of 12 half-grown, back-stabbing boys, but some of the problems can seem just as bad. Consider these complications:

• Many children of divorce suffer from prolonged, aching grief over the breakup of their homes. Sometimes they silently shed tears late in the night; other times, the grief is repressed. Frequently their sorrow is softened by a secret hope that their parents will get back together. This fantasy (as psychologists call it) is shattered when a stepparent walks into their lives. All hope now gone, the child's grief becomes anger and, whether repressed or expressed, can lead to a long period of underlying stress between child and adult.

• Additionally, many children of divorce bond more tightly than usual with their custodial parent, usually their mother. They've gone through the divorce crisis together, becoming "foxhole buddies." The child views the stepparent as a threat to that exclusive relationship. The relationships overlapping between birth parents, stepparents, and children are far more emotionally-complicated than corresponding relationships in many traditional homes.

• Often stepparents come into their new situation with high hopes, ready to assume instant parenthood, and eager to be loved and accepted by the children. If two sets of children are involved, the two spouses long for the two halves of their lives to blend together as normally and instantly as the Brady Bunch. Stepparents with these expectations are almost always disappointed, and the resulting feelings of rejection are hard for many stepparents to accept.

• The bonding relationship between stepparent and stepchild is further complicated by frequent animosity and rivalry with the non-custodial biological parent. Visitation rights and financial arrangements with the ex-spouse frequently seep into the existing marriage and cause turmoil in the home. Parents who remain involved in post-divorce, emotional wars not only harm the child, they deeply damage the blending processes of the new families.

• Another problem occurs whenever a new stepparent senses his or her spouse siding with the children. Becky had divorced her first husband Stevie when Traci was two years old, and propelled by guilt she "spoiled" Traci, spending vast amounts of money on her, trying to "make up" for the divorce. She and Traci had lived together for six years ("just the two of us") when she married Jack, and he found himself unwelcomed by his new stepdaughter. When an argument arose shortly afterward, Traci blew up at her stepfather. She said that he had ruined everything, that she hated him, and that he would "never ever" be her father. When she punctuated her remarks by some profanity she'd heard at school, Jack returned the fire. Becky had never before allowed anyone to speak sharply to her little girl, and before she realized it, she drew Traci beside her. Putting her arm tightly around her, she took her side in the argument.

• Consider also the awkwardness of two sets of children suddenly coming together as instant brothers and sisters. It's bad enough with younger children who frequently don't like one another on general principle. But it's even more difficult in the case of older children who find themselves liking each other too much. Seventeen-year-old Eric, for example, was handsome, well-built, and breezy. He frequently worked in the yard without his shirt and seldom wore much clothing in his bedroom. His new half-sister Brandy found herself sexually attracted to him. Brandy, furthermore, was well-developed herself and she liked to sunbathe in the back yard. Eric was definitely aroused by her but hadn't a clue as to how to handle the situation.

• Even more difficult are the sexual feelings that frequently arise between stepparents and their non-biological teenage stepchild.

• Some of the biggest conflicts in stepfamilies often occur between teenage daughters and their new stepmothers. In fact, whenever remarriage occurs in a home containing a teenage daughter, there's a high potential for stress.

• Many frustrations stem from raising kids in two environments with two sets of values. One parent told me, "What takes us two weeks to establish is messed up in one day after she's been with her dad. How can we be good examples to her when she has to go back every other weekend into that other environment where there's no discipline?"

Atop all these problems are the financial pressures that often befall stepfamilies. Only 37 percent of stepfamilies have household incomes of $50,000, compared with 45 percent of traditional families. "I don't mind his children coming over every other weekend," said one mother with two children of her own. "But six of us in a two-bedroom apartment is just too hard. I wish we could afford a larger place, but his alimony and child-support payments are too high. His ex-wife is a witch, and she has us just where she wants us—in the poor house." These problems are complicated by the tendency of husbands and wives to keep their assets separated to protect their own biological children's future needs. Healthcare, insurance, and legal rights also become difficult to sort out in divorced/remarried situations.

Another problem seems smaller, but can cause anxiety for children in the family: what to call the new stepparent and how to refer to him or her in front of friends. "Tim, I'd like you to meet Jonathan ... er, my dad ... er, my stepdad ... er, my mom's new husband."

 Let's Talk: **Did you grow up in a stepfamily? Are you currently in a stepfamily or blended family? What challenges do you face that other families might not? What opportunities or advantages do you have?**

For all these reasons and more, many psychologists say that stepfamilies are nothing at all like traditional families. Increasing numbers of second marriages and blended families fail. About 50 percent of remarried couples with children end up in another divorce according to sociologist Paul Glick.[3]

They don't have to.

In most cases, the problems can be converted into opportunities for growth and grace, resulting in closer and happier home life than most family members dreamed. The attitudes recorded at the beginning of this chapter can become the norm in stepfamilies.

How? Well, it helps just knowing the problems. The ones I've mentioned are common to most stepfamilies, and if you're encountering some of them, realize that you're not alone. These problems can be handled and even overcome.

A Quadrangle of Scriptures

At the risk of sounding overly simplistic, I'd like to suggest a quadrangle of Scriptures to surround the blended family. **Passage number one** is Ephesians 2:13-14: "Now in Christ Jesus you who once were far away have been brought near through the blood of Christ. For he himself is our peace, who has made the two one and has destroyed the barrier, the dividing wall of hostility."

Christ Jesus specializes in turning failures into successes and uniting fragments into wholes. His death on the cross not only provided a basis for bringing us together with the Heavenly Father, it provided the potential for bringing us together with one another. In this passage, the apostle Paul was addressing the division between Jews and Gentiles, two groups who by nature and habit were distant from each other.

Paul insisted that the blood of Christ could make them one in heart and spirit, for Christ's power is the basis of peace and unity. Christ takes two opposites and melts down the barriers between them, dismantles the dividing wall of hostility, and enables two to become one.

The implications of this truth for members of a blended family are profound. The greatest contribution you can make toward uniting your stepfamily is personally committing yourself fully to Jesus Christ and becoming a spiritual source of prayer, patience, and maturity in your home. Begin reading the Bible each day, memorizing verses you find that relate to your family. Intercede with God each day in the privacy of your room or car, praying for each member of your family. And resolve, with God's help, to release bitterness and resentment, to forgive those who have hurt you, and to control your temper when provoked. Ask God to give you the wisdom he promises, for James 1:5 says, "If any of you lacks wisdom, he should ask God, who gives generously to all without finding fault, and it will be given him."

Ideally, the decision to follow Jesus Christ will be shared by your new spouse and by each member of the household. But if not, don't underestimate the influence you can have as the presence of Christ radiates from your heart into your home. Harold Bloomfield wrote:

In an ideal world, you and your spouse work ... together to make peace in your stepfamily. In the real world, you may be the one most concerned, and it may take considerable time to enlist your spouse's full support. It is important to recognize at this early stage in your efforts to heal stepfamily conflict that you do have the power alone to make a significant difference. You can initiate profound change that will accelerate positively if you take the first steps.

Other people's behavior depends as much or more on the emotional environment you generate as on their personality traits.

Making peace in your stepfamily begins with you.[4]

Scripture Search: **Read Ephesians 2:14-16.**

For he himself is our peace, who has made the two one and has destroyed the barrier, the dividing wall of hostility ... His purpose was to create in himself one new man out of the two, thus making peace, and in this one body to reconcile both of them to God through the cross, by which he put to death their hostility.

√ Complete the sentence: Hostility and division can only be genuinely overcome by ...
- ❑ a positive attitude
- ❑ passively giving in
- ❑ the cross of Christ
- ❑ psychology

Ephesians 4 is the **second passage** in my quadrangle. It provides the practical applications of the theological truths of Ephesians 1–3.

Read the following verses in Ephesians 4 and rate their relevance to blended families. In front of each verse, write *very relevant, relevant,* or *not very relevant.*

Be completely humble and gentle; be patient, bearing with one another in love (v. 2).

Speaking the truth in love, we will in all things grow up into him who is the Head, that is, Christ (v. 15).

Each of you must put off falsehood and speak truthfully to his neighbor, for we are all members of one body (v. 25).

In your anger do not sin. Do not let the sun go down while you are still angry, and do not give the devil a foothold (vv. 26-27).

Do not let any unwholesome talk come out of your mouths, but only what is helpful for building others up according to their needs (v. 29).

Do not grieve the Holy Spirit of God, with which you were sealed for the day of redemption (vs. 30).

Get rid of all bitterness, rage and anger, brawling and slander, along with every form of malice. Be kind and compassionate to one another, forgiving each other, just as in Christ God forgave you (v. 31-32).

Blending a family takes time. Most of us believe in "love at first sight." We think romance or friendship occurs because "there's chemistry between us," or because "we just clicked." That's not realistic in traditional relationships; in stepfamilies, it almost never happens. Expectations of instant love need to be replaced by long-term efforts at nurturing friendships and molding relationships. Stepfamily relationships are like a bridge; they have to be built one step at a time.

Most social scientists stress this point above all others in their writings about stepfamilies. They also report that while stepfamilies experience a great deal of trouble their first two years, they often grow more stable than traditional first-marriage homes after five years. It takes time to accept change, time to adjust to new people. Psychologist Patricia Papernow, Ed.D., author of *Becoming a Stepfamily,* says that it takes "three to seven years for any stepfamily to fully bond."[5] John and Emily Visher, a psychiatrist-psychologist team who have worked extensively with blended families, claim that it takes 18 to 24 months to establish a cordial relationship with stepchildren."[6]

I hope knowing the blending process takes time encourages you to persevere. Stresses and confrontations early in the process are common, but parents and stepparents who are anchored in Christ have access to the emotional resources to keep working on the relationships.

Persevering means taking time for your marriage, for the emotional stability in stepfamilies as well as in first-marriage families depends on the strength of the husband and wife relationship.

Persevering means under-reacting to a stepchild's hostility, absorbing a certain amount of pain, and responding to provocation with patience, knowing that time is your ally. Children must form relationships at their own pace. One stepmother told me, "I've wanted to hug my two older stepchildren, but I haven't yet. They've accepted me, but without the hugging part. I feel uncomfortable not knowing if I should initiate it or wait for them. But," she added, "I can see it starting to happen."

Persevering means spending enough one-on-one time in relaxed settings with your child or stepchild for the defenses to lower and barriers to fall. Proverbs 20:5 can be paraphrased as, "The purposes of a child's heart are deep waters, but a parent of understanding draws them out." Experts disagree on whether the stepparent should assume a "buddy" role or a "parent" role, but in either case, it's important to go to ball games together, shop, fish, or out for pizza and a movie, and as frequently as possible.

Persevering means establishing fair and consistent family rules, and sticking to them without partiality. This requires the couple to talk through parenting issues with openness, honesty, and tolerance.

Persevering means establishing new traditions for the family like camping in the backyard, spending Fridays at the water park or Saturdays at the ballpark, going to the beach every July, finding unique ways to celebrate holidays, and playing touch football every other weekend when extra siblings are added to the "home" team.

Persevering means reading about stepfamily issues and perhaps joining a Christian-based support group for blended families.

Persevering means a pit-bull determination to succeed, to press on, to do your part, and radiate hope even when problems arise and tension fills the air like an electrical storm.

The **third passage** I'd suggest for empowered stepparenting is the simple beatitude Jesus gave us in Matthew 5:9, "Blessed are the peacemakers, for they will be called sons of God."

Empowered stepparents are by necessity diplomats, and while they must frequently ply this trade among their stepchildren, the most difficult peacemaking involves the ex-spouse. Few divorces end in friendship, and post-divorce conflicts can pollute the new home like sewers draining into a lake. When an ex-spouse is victimizing, vindictive, and interfering, the temptation to retaliate is intense. It takes incredible self-control to remain civil, to speak well of the former spouse in front of the children, and to avoid using the kids as the rope in a tug-of-war.

Peacemakers are not overly passive, allowing themselves to be abused or exploited. Peacemakers do practice Proverbs 29:11:

> A fool gives full vent to his anger,
> but a wise man keeps himself under control.

The biggest source of problems for kids in stepfamilies is parental conflict left over from the prior marriage. The welfare of the children (and to an extent the success of the blended family) requires peacemaking with the ex-spouse—at least as far as the youngsters are concerned. "If it is possible," wrote the apostle Paul, "as far as it depends on you, live at peace with everyone" (Romans 12:18).

The **final passage** I'm suggesting for blended families is found in the middle of the Bible's most mournful book. The weeping prophet Jeremiah wrote his Lamentations, grieving over the death of his nation Israel and its capital Jerusalem. But in the middle of his moaning, he added: "Because of the Lord's great love we are not consumed, for his compassions never fail. They are new every morning; great is your faithfulness" (Lamentations 3:22-23).

47

The first person to invent the wheel only discovered what God had already designed, for the Lord created things in circles. The stars and planets are round, they move in orbital circuits, and life, as a result, moves in cycles. Every 365 days, we have a new year; every 24 hours we have a new day; every 60 minutes we have a new hour. God created the potential for new beginnings into the very design of our universe.

If you're starting marriage over, if you're trying to establish a new home, if you're seeking to blend two families into one ...

—give yourself to Christ, asking Him to break down walls of hostility.

—persevere, remembering that it takes extraordinary effort and considerable time to adjust, to accept, and to build deeply-loving relationships in blended families.

—do your best to live at peace with your ex-spouse.

—remind yourself frequently of God's unfailing mercy and love; he's even more concerned about your family than you are, and He shares your burden ...

... for His compassions never fail, they are new every morning. Great is His faithfulness!

P.S. (Practical Suggestions from Chapter 4)

1. If you are nursing a bitter or resentful attitude toward your ex-spouse, ask God to deal with you about it. It often helps to write down the offenses and incidents that have hurt you. Read your list to the Lord in prayer before burning it or washing it down the drain. Entrust your former mate into God's hands. Let the Lord assume responsibility for any conviction or vengeance that may be appropriate. Turn the last five verses of Romans 12 into a prayer for yourself, praying it to the Lord every day if necessary.

2. Sit down with your new spouse (and perhaps your entire family) and brainstorm about family traditions. Select some activities, habits, or hobbies that will involve the entire family, and begin using them to make memories that will last a lifetime.

3. Ask your children to each write a letter to the Lord, describing their feelings about being in a blended family. Tell them to be honest about their hurts, their anger, their disappointment, and their hopes. You might share with them a similar letter of your own, letting them know some of your struggles. But tell them that their letter is a private one, and that you will never read it unless they agree. Seal each letter in an individual envelope, and write over the seal the words of Lamentations 3:22-23.

4. With your spouse, make a list of ways to simplify your lifestyle. Blended families are hectic homes, especially on weekends when all the children are together. Develop specific steps to uncomplicate

your schedule, allowing you to plan ahead, be organized, and invest sufficient time in building relationships with the children.

5. Select a good book on stepparenting. Read it carefully, acquainting yourself with the challenges and opportunities of building your new team from your assortment of individual players.

6. Have a weekend retreat with your spouse. Choose a spot you both enjoy. In this pleasant, relaxed environment, come to agreement on matters like discipline, what the children should call you, and establishing family devotions.

7. In your daily Bible study, read through the book of Proverbs and mark every verse that describes a character quality you need for effective stepparenting. Memorize some of those verses, and put them into practice.

8. Gather other blended family couples and form a support group in your home or church based on *New Faces in the Frame: A Guide to Marriage and Parenting in the Blended Family* by Dick Dunn. This 12-week study is divided into two parts. The first part studies the new marriage relationship. Part 2 covers stepparenting issues. This will provide a welcome forum for couples to air their concerns and gather new insights as they fellowship with others traveling the stepparenting road. *New Faces in the Frame* (item #7200-65) is available at your local Baptist Book Store or Lifeway Christian Store or by calling 1-800-458-2772.

[1]Harold H. Bloomfield, *Making Peace in Your Stepfamily* (New York: Hyperion, 1993), 25.
[2]Jan Larson, "Understanding Stepfamilies," *American Demographics,* July 1992, 36.
[3]Ibid., 40.
[4]Bloomfield, *Making Peace in Your Stepfamily,* 20-21.
[5]Myriam Weisang Misrach, "The Wicked Stepmother and Other Nasty Myths: The Truth About What It Really Takes to Be a Stepfamily," *Redbook,* July 1993, 89.
[6]Ibid., 90.

Stages in the Journey

Get a Head Start on Parenting

The Crucial, Crazy Preschool Years

Raising Confident Elementary-Age Kids

The Joy of Raising Teenagers

∞ 5 ∞
Get a Head Start on Parenting

As we circled the island, the tour guide told us, "Manhattan actually weighs less now than it did 200 years ago." Seeing our surprise, she explained that construction crews must excavate deeply when building skyscrapers. The amount of stone removed is heavier than all the building materials brought in. "A very deep foundation is necessary for a very tall building," she said, "and it must be laid in the very earliest stages before any structure appears to human eyes."

It's the same with kids.

A current psychology textbook puts it plainly, "The first months of life, from conception through birth, can be considered the most critical of the entire life span. Not only is growth more rapid and the developing person more vulnerable than at any other time, but the role of other people is more crucial."[1]

New appreciation for quality prenatal parenting is emerging in the United States, a yearning to provide strong foundations for children at their earliest stages. *American Demographics* recently reported that the number of companies providing prenatal healthcare benefits to their employees has increased dramatically as companies have learned prenatal care costs less than the costs of childbirth without such care.[2]

Fewer medications are now available to pregnant women, as doctors learn more about the sensitivity of the preborn to substances in their mothers' systems. Smoking around mothers-to-be has become taboo, and experts warn that even trace amounts of illicit drugs can irreparably harm the fetus.

It shouldn't surprise us that the Bible was ahead of its time on this issue. Many Scriptures, beginning with the Mosaic laws, emphasize God's concern for the preborn child.

The Lord said to Jeremiah:

" 'Before I formed you in the womb I knew you,
      before you were born I set you apart' " (Jeremiah 1:5).

And the psalmist wrote:

You made all the delicate, inner parts of my body, and knit them together in my mother's womb. Thank you for making me so wonderfully complex! It is amazing to think about. Your workmanship is marvelous—and how well I know it. You were there while I was being formed in utter seclusion! You saw me before I was born and scheduled each day of my life before I began to breathe (Psalm 139:13-16, TLB).

Scripture Search: **Read the selected passages below from Psalm 139. They offer praise to God for His care before and after birth.**

O Lord, you have searched me
　　and you know me.
You know when I sit and when I rise;
　　you perceive my thoughts from afar ...
Before a word is on my tongue
　　you know it completely, O Lord.

You hem me in—behind and before;
　　you have laid your hand upon me ...

Where can I go from your Spirit?
　　Where can I flee from your presence?
If I go up to the heavens, you are there;
　　if I make my bed in the depths, you are there ...

If I say, "Surely the darkness will hide me
　　and the light become night around me,"
even the darkness will not be dark to you; ...
　　for darkness is as light to you.

For you created my inmost being;
　　you knit me together in my mother's womb.
I praise you because I am fearfully and wonderfully made; ...
My frame was not hidden from you
　　when I was made in the secret place.
When I was woven together in the depths of the earth,
　　your eyes saw my unformed body.
All the days ordained for me
　　were written in your book
　　before one of them came to be.

Based on these verses, label these statements *true* or *false:*
_____ God's concern for us begins at birth.
_____ God plans each day of our lives in advance.
_____ God sees us in our mothers' wombs.
_____ We can hide from the Lord.
_____ God can read our minds.

Wonderfully Complex

We now know that within 3 weeks of conception, before most women even realize they're pregnant, the baby's heart begins to beat. By the 6th week the adrenal and thyroid glands are functioning, and there is even measurable brain function. By the 12th week a child's fingerprints are distinct, unique, and identifiable.

Within three months all organ systems are functioning. He can breathe, swallow, digest and eliminate, sleep, awaken, hear, taste, and feel. By the fourth month his face shows distinctive features. Hair, eyebrows, and eyelashes begin to grow. By the fifth and sixth months he can recognize sounds from outside the womb, and his eyes can perceive light and darkness from the outside world.

All the great advances of medicine and science in understanding prenatal life are but commentary and validation of what the Bible said three thousand years ago: "We are fearfully and wonderfully made" (Psalm 139:14, KJV).

But biblical truth about the preborn also has powerful implications in another area—parenting. Wise prenatal parenting can start our children with a leg up in the world before they even begin to walk!

The Bible's Best Example

Aged Zechariah and Elizabeth had missed the cooing and crying of a baby in their home, for they were infertile, a condition considered a disgrace among the ancient Hebrews. But an angel appeared to Zechariah by the altar in Jerusalem's temple, telling him his prayers had been heard. What prayers? Petitions offered years before by a young couple for a baby. Prayers never answered.

Until now.

> The angel said to him, "Do not be afraid, Zecharias, for your petition has been heard, and your wife Elisabeth will bear you a son and you will give him the name John. And you will have joy and gladness, and many will rejoice at his birth. For he will be great in the sight of the Lord, and he will drink no wine or liquor; and he will be filled with the Holy Spirit, while yet in his mother's womb" (Luke 1:13-15, NASB).

Zechariah stammered his doubts and lost his tongue. As the news spread, the neighbors were astonished. Elizabeth, old and pregnant, went into seclusion, hiding herself five months. In the sixth month she received a visitor, the pregnant virgin Mary. When Elizabeth heard Mary's greeting, John leapt in her womb, and Elizabeth was filled with the Holy Spirit (see Luke 1:39-41).

This story highlights three important prenatal parenting concerns.

The Physical Care for the Preborn

A pregnant woman should take care of herself physically. She needs to eat a healthy, balanced diet, for current research demonstrates that a child's resistance to infection for the first 18 years of life is bolstered by good nutrition in the womb. She needs to avoid smoking, smoke-filled environments, alcohol, and drugs; and she needs to exercise.

Elizabeth must have done all these things, not just when she was pregnant, but throughout her life. How else would she have been able to handle her pregnancy in old age? John's birth is no less God's miracle when we give Elizabeth credit for being physically ready. All her life she had prayed for a child, and when his coming was announced, she had no need for lifestyle and diet changes. She was ready.

 Let's Talk: **Why is it often hard for an expectant mom to stay in good physical shape? How can her husband and her friends help?**

The Emotional Care for the Preborn

Elizabeth was elderly, well past child-bearing years, and this pregnancy was supernatural. Everyone must have whispered the news in astonishment. The stress of it all may have been what sent Elizabeth into seclusion for the first five months. The following three months were spent in quiet fellowship with her friend and relative, Mary.

A recent article, "Second-Hand Stress," says, "newborns suffer when mothers-to-be experience chronic anxiety and distress. Maternal stress can increase the likelihood of prematurity and lower-than-normal birth weight."[3]

It stands to reason. A baby picks up his mother's moods like no one else ever can or will. Babies suffer before they're born if their home is filled with anger, fighting, and tension. But the impact of a wholesome Christian environment—a happy home, a singing mother, a praying family—provides a nine-month head start on a victorious life. The mother who knows how to relax, trusting God with the pressures of life, will be healthier, and so will her child.

 Let's Talk: **Are you in a crisis pregnancy right now? What can you or others do to reduce the tension you and your preborn child are feeling?**

The Spiritual Care for the Preborn

Luke 1:41 says, "When Elizabeth heard Mary's greeting, the baby leaped in her womb, and Elizabeth was filled with the Holy Spirit." Verse 44 reports Elizabeth's testimony: "As soon as the sound of your greeting reached my ears, the baby in my womb leaped for joy." We know preborn babies hear sounds outside the womb by the sixth month.

My interest in this subject began when I heard a report that some newborns show signs of recognizing the musical themes of the soap operas their mothers watched during the latter months of pregnancy. I thought, "Why couldn't babies recognize hymns and Scripture songs?"

It makes a powerful, lifetime impact on a person—don't you think?— if a preborn child hears his father and mother praying together; if he hears them singing songs of praise and worship together; if he hears them reading aloud the Word of God; if he hears the sound of Christian music in the home from stereo or radio; if he hears a worshiping congregation singing praises to the Lord all around him.

The Greek word for the unborn baby in verses 41 and 44 is the same word translated *infancy* in 2 Timothy 3:15: "From infancy you have known the holy Scriptures." I believe a home's spiritual atmosphere can be sensed in the womb. After all, "When Elizabeth heard Mary's greeting, the baby leaped in her womb, and Elizabeth was filled with the Holy Spirit" (v. 41). Mary's visit to Elizabeth represented more than physical companionship or emotional support. It was God's special confirmation that He was working in and through her life to accomplish His redemptive purpose. I'm not surprised that Elizabeth felt overwhelmed with the presence and power of the Holy Spirit *or* that John sensed in the womb the intensity of his mother's spiritual experience.

Scripture Search: Read Ephesians 5:18-21.

Do not get drunk with wine, for that is dissipation, but be filled with the Spirit, speaking to one another in psalms and hymns and spiritual songs, singing and making melody with your heart to the Lord; always giving thanks for all things in the name of our Lord Jesus Christ to God, even the Father; and be subject to one another in the fear of Christ (NASB).

Based on these verses, what specific qualities should be exhibited in those who are Spirit-filled? ✓ Check all that apply.

❑ Drunkenness   ❑ Singing
❑ Irritability   ❑ Anxiety
❑ Thanksgiving   ❑ A humble, submissive attitude

Imagine counseling expectant parents. List three recommendations to enhance their spiritual health.

1. _____

2. _____

3. _____

When my wife became pregnant with our first child, I knew it before she did. She was too sick to drive to the doctor's office, so I took the "sample" and heard the report. Driving home, I was filled with mixed emotions. I was floating on a cloud of joy, but it was streaked with worry. I didn't have a job to support a family. I had worked here and there, waiting for a church to invite me to pastor, and Katrina had supported us by working in a discount store. I had interviewed with a dozen churches, but none of them had called me. I turned on the radio, and a song filled the car, an old gospel song I'll never forget.

> *Be not dismayed, what 'ere betide*
> > *God will take care of you.*
> *Beneath his wings of love abide*
> > *God will take care of you.* [4]

By the time Victoria was born, we were serving a picture-postcard church near the Smoky Mountains. We had a cozy home, adequate income, new friends. All our needs were met. Victoria, even before birth, was wrapped in the care of God.

John, too, began the race before him in pole position because his parents knew the spiritual secrets of prenatal care.

Since life begins at conception, we must assume parenting begins there, too. Get a nine-month head start, and your children will one day testify as the psalmist did long ago:

> *Oh yes, you shaped me first inside, then out;*
> > *you formed me in my mother's womb. ...*
> *You know exactly how I was made, bit by bit,*
> > *how I was sculpted from nothing into something.*
> *Like an open book, you watched me grow from conception*
> > *to birth;*
> > *all the stages of my life were spread out before you.* [5]

P.S. (Practical Suggestions from Chapter 5)

If you're an expectant parent:
- Play uplifting Christian recordings throughout the day.
- Begin a family devotional time. Spend a few minutes each day reading the Scripture and praying aloud.
- Be involved in your church during your pregnancy. The impact of a worshiping environment on a preborn baby may be significant. Make church attendance a habit before the baby is born; it's difficult to do so amid the changes and transitions of the postnatal period.
- Avoid smoke-filled environments; obey the prenatal instructions of your gynecologist. Eat and exercise according to guidelines.
- Avoid loud, violence-centered entertainment.
- Ask several people to pray daily for you, your child, and your home.

[1]Kathleen Stassen Berger, *The Developing Person Through the Life Span* (New York: Worth Publishers, Inc., 1988), 77.

[2]"Prenatal Programs Pay Off," Health Care, *American Demographics*, February 1991, 14.

[3]Andrea Bauman, "Second-Hand Stress," *American Health*, April 1991, 74.

[4]Civilla D. Martin, "God Will Take Care of You," *The Baptist Hymnal*, © Copyright 1991, Convention Press. All rights reserved. International copyright secured. Used by permission.

[5]Eugene H. Peterson, *The Message: Psalms* (Colorado Springs: NavPress, 1994), 187.

∼ 6 ∼

The Crazy, Crucial Preschool Years

Empowered Parenting began with Moses' words to parents in Deuteronomy. Moses also wrote a song for parents—Psalm 90—that stresses the importance of the early childhood years. Evidently written near the end of Moses' life, it begins,
> "Lord, you have been our dwelling place
>> throughout all generations" (Psalm 90:1).

Then he speaks of the brevity of life, about 70 or 80 years on average, and of its labor and sorrow; for it is soon cut off, and we fly away.

For the Christian, that's a glad prediction rather than a sad pronouncement. We're strangers and pilgrims on earth, looking for a city whose builder and maker is God. Because our earthly lives are so brief, we must live them carefully, using every moment to full advantage for the Master. So Moses prayed:
> "Teach us to number our days aright,
>> that we may gain a heart of wisdom" (Psalm 90:12).

And how do parents teach their youngsters to present the Savior a heart of wisdom? Moses said:
> "Satisfy us in the morning [that is, in the morning of life]
>> with your unfailing love,
> that we may sing for joy and be glad all our days"
>>>> (Psalm 90:14).

In other words, if a child's heart is satisfied in early childhood with the unfailing love of God, he'll "sing for joy and be glad" all his days. Moses knew, as modern experts now affirm, that the preschool years are critical to the development of a person's life and personality. "During no other period of life is the person so transformed both physically and developmentally as during infancy."[1] Christian psychiatrist, Paul D. Meier, says, "It is my firm belief that approximately 85 percent of one's adult personality is formed by the time he is six years old. Those first six years, therefore, are obviously the most crucial."[2]

A classic Old Testament story beautifully illustrates this principle—the story of Elkanah, his wife Hannah, and their child, Samuel.

A Visit to an Old Testament Home

Elkanah was a God-fearing, gentle man who lived in a beautiful section of the Jordan valley of central Israel. He seemed tender, faithful, generous, and pious. He fell in love with a gutsy, godly woman whose name, Hannah, meant *grace*.

Hannah and Elkanah grieved for they were unable to have children. They suffered deeply, and their infertility haunted them day and night. So according the custom of the time, Elkanah finally turned to a surrogate mother to provide him heirs. This naturally complicated their simple home, especially because surrogate Peninnah resented Elkanah's obvious love for Hannah. Peninnah had no problem bearing children, and she and her passel of kids taunted Hannah with daily insults.

Hannah earnestly prayed for a child. Finally God answered her with a precious boy she named Samuel, meaning *answered prayer*.

But "Grace" didn't keep "Answered Prayer" at home very long. When Samuel was fully weaned (perhaps three to five years old in those days!), Hannah and Elkanah took him to the house of God at Shiloh, dedicated him to the Lord, and left him to grow up among the priests of Israel. Samuel became one of the greatest heroes of the Old Testament. He grew up secure and strong enough to fill the political and spiritual vacuum of his nation, becoming the last of the judges, the first of the prophets, and the anointer of kings.

How, then, did Elkanah and Hannah raise their preschooler? Earlier we studied the ABCs for a solid marriage. Now consider the ABCs of raising preschoolers.

A = Attitude

Attitude precedes technique. Most parenting books emphasize technique, but methods without maturity are dangerous. Hannah cultivated three areas of attitudinal maturity, clearly described in 1 Samuel 1.

A patient attitude. Notice her response to the stresses she encountered:

> *Because the Lord had closed her womb, her rival kept provoking her in order to irritate her. This went on year after year. Whenever Hannah went up to the house of the Lord, her rival provoked her till she wept and would not eat. ... In bitterness of soul, Hannah wept much and prayed to the Lord (1 Samuel 1:6-7,10).*

Hannah endured years of verbal and emotional abuse under her own roof from her husband's second family. I would have declared war, developed strategy, stockpiled ammunition, deployed troops, fired missiles, screamed, threatened, and buried Peninnah under a barrage of counterabuse. But Hannah remained in firmer control of her temper, and, though saddened, brought her problems and pressures to the Lord.

That patience undoubtedly served her well when little Samuel was born and she had to raise him amid dangerous times in a little house filled with her husband's concubine and kids.

Even under the best of circumstances, it takes a lot of patience to raise preschoolers. Nancy Samalin, in her book *Love and Anger: The Parental Dilemma* confesses, "I never even knew I had a temper until I had children."[3]

Childhood magazine recently reported:

> *What was the leading cause of death from injury during the first year of life in the United States? Drowning? No. House fires? Guess again. Suffocation? Aspiration of food or objects? Motor vehicle accidents? None of these lead the list. ... The leading cause of injury deaths—17 percent of such deaths—for children under a year of age in the United States in the first half of the 1980s ... was homicide. This, of course, is only the tip of the iceberg of infant abuse.*[4]

As horrifying as that statement is, it's even more horrible to admit that most of us who have raised infants and preschoolers can understand it a bit. Nothing tries the patience of an exhausted dad who has to go to work at 6:00 a.m. more than an infant who screams and cries hours on end during the wee hours of the night. Nothing exasperates a weary mother like the destructive energy of a two-year-old tornado relentlessly spinning at 300 mph from one end of the house to another, upending everything in sight.

Many parents who wouldn't dream of physically abusing their children unwittingly are verbally abusive, and they're just as destructive. Proverbs 18:21 warns, "The tongue has the power of life and death." Harsh words inflict irreparable harm and may damage a child as deeply as physical abuse. Correct children's behavior, but never shred their self-worth.

Here are some words parents should never use:

> *"You're nothing but a problem."*
> *"You're sorry, just like your dad."*
> *"I wish you'd never been born."*
> *"You can't do anything right."*
> *"You'll never amount to anything."*
> *"How can you be so stupid?"*
> *"I'm so tired of you I could scream."*

 Let's Talk: How well did your parents manage their tempers? Were you the object of abuse? What techniques do you use to manage your anger when stressed by parenting?

How can we develop the kind of patience Hannah seemed to have?

1. Patience comes with maturity, and maturity comes with cultivating your daily relationship with Jesus. Make certain that you have a firm commitment to Christ as your Lord and Master.

2. Ask God for patience. Many times we haven't the things we need because we've failed to sincerely ask for them (see James 4:2).

3. Patience is a decision, so choose self-control even when you're most provoked. All the major Christian attitudes—love, joy, peace, patience, and the others in Galatians 5:22—involve the element of

choice. You can decide, as the Holy Spirit empowers you, to love, to rejoice, and to remain tranquil and patient.

Susannah Wesley is revered in church history for her mothering skills. One day her husband remarked, "I wonder at your patience. You have told the same thing to that child twenty times."

"Had I satisfied myself by saying the matter only nineteen times," Susannah replied, "I should have lost all my labor. You see, it was the twentieth time that crowned the whole."[5]

Scripture Search: **Read the selected passages from Proverbs below. In the first blank in each verse, write what you think is the most appropriate word. After you have completed all the verses, look each one up and write the actual biblical word in the second blank. Circle each verse in which your word closely matched the actual term.**

A _____ / _____ man has great understanding,
but a quick-tempered man displays folly (Proverbs 14:29).

A hot-tempered man stirs up dissension,
but a patient man _____ / _____ a quarrel
(Proverbs 15:18).

Better a patient man than a warrior,
a man who controls his _____ / _____
than one who takes a city (Proverbs 16:32).

A man of knowledge uses words with restraint,
and a man of understanding is _____ / _____
(Proverbs 17:27).

A _____ / _____ gives full vent to his anger,
but a wise man keeps himself under control
(Proverbs 29:11).

4. Making a strategic exit is vital for parents who might otherwise verbally or physically abuse their children. When you feel yourself losing control, leave the room. Separate yourself from the provocation, take a deep breath, and master the emotions rushing to the forefront.

5. Learn key Bible verses on the subject of patience, such as those in the Scripture Search you just completed. Incredible power surges through the living Word of God. When you memorize and meditate on

Scripture, the energy of the Holy Spirit is activated in your life, and God helps you develop the mature patience you need as a parent.

There's another reason to control your temper. A toddler doesn't have a well-developed ability to handle his emotions, and so he badly needs you to handle yours. When a two- or three-year-old becomes angry, he's angry all over, top to toe, and has limited ability to control it. When you face the force of a child's tantrum, what do you do?

First, *stay as calm as you can.* When your child gets overheated, he needs you to stay cool. What a child needs most when he's out of control is an adult who isn't!

Second, *let children express a certain amount of anger.* They need to vent negative emotions. If you're at home, you can walk away or lead him to his room. He'll learn a tantrum is no fun when no one is there.

But you're likely to be in a public place—a grocery store, for example, or on an airplane. Go to your car or to a restroom, and let the tantrum run its course. You might have to leave your shopping cart in the middle of the aisle, but that's all right. At that moment, your child needs you more than you need a pound of hamburger. Hold him like you normally do to comfort him, in spite of the squirming or flailing about he's doing. This prevents him from hurting himself or becoming destructive. If you're in a public situation, don't worry about what other people are thinking. All that matters at that point is your child.

Third, *don't reward his tantrum by giving in to it.* You'll reinforce a destructive pattern and teach him that anger will get him what he wants. I've worked recently with a couple whose four-year-old is out of control. By one-and-a-half, he'd learned that he could manipulate his parents by temper tantrums. His venue of choice was screaming. Then he progressed to beating his head against the wall, guaranteed to inflict massive parental guilt and distress. Now, he slaps his parents and verbally abuses them. He screams, "I don't love you any more," and hits them. At four years old, he knows anger gets him whatever he wants.

You're not doing your child a favor when you reward his tantrum by giving in to it.

 Let's Talk: How did you respond to a recent temper tantrum thrown by your preschooler? What helped you deal with your child's anger?

Finally, *talk to your child about his feelings.* It's likely that your child has exhausted himself. Exhaustion, in fact, probably contributed to his tantrum; so help him rest. Rock him, sing quiet songs, hug and kiss him, reassure him he's safe. An older preschooler then can talk with you about how he felt. Later, when he's refreshed, show him a verse in your Bible about anger and help him memorize a key phrase.

Everyone needs a temper. Temper gives knives their flexibility. Temper gives steel its strength. The word *temper* means a moderate, flexible, strong-yet-relaxed spirit, the ability to bend without breaking. Good tempers make healthy homes.

A prayerful attitude. Hannah demonstrated such a prayerful attitude that half of all verses about her in the Old Testament describe her at prayer. Her patience was borne of her prayerfulness; her refuge was the throne of grace.

Hannah wept much and prayed to the Lord. In her anguish, she promised God that if He gave her a son, she would give him back for the ministry. This vow is very precious to me, for I'm also the son of such a prayer. My parents, after a heartbreaking miscarriage, were advised they couldn't have children. But they earnestly prayed, promising God that if He gave them a son, they would dedicate him to the gospel ministry. Thus I was born, and in the course of time I became a pastor. My mother told me this after I entered the ministry. Throughout my childhood, I felt no pressure from my parents to enter this vocation. In fact, at times I felt they sought to discourage me.

Notice that in 1 Samuel chapter 1, Hannah prayed for her child before his birth, and in chapter 2, she prayed for him after his birth. Prayer is perhaps our greatest tool for child-rearing, for it brings the power of highest heaven to bear upon our children's lives. Church history is written from the prayers of parents. It's well known that St. Augustine was converted in response to his mother's persistent prayers. Less known is a similar story of another woman who prayed for her son as she labored at her washboard day after day, her tears falling in the soapy water. Her boy John, a teenage runaway, had reportedly become a wicked man. But her prayers for him were ceaseless, and as she scrubbed at her washboard, the Lord washed his heart and saved him. John Newton later described his conversion with these words:

> *Amazing grace, how sweet the sound*
> *That saved a wretch like me.*
> *I once was lost, but now I'm found*
> *Was blind, but now I see.*[6]

Among the many people converted to Christ through Newton's ministry was Thomas Scott who became a well-known Christian minister. He won, among others, William Cowper, who later wrote:

> *There is a fountain filled with blood*
> *Drawn from Immanuel's veins,*
> *And sinners, plunged beneath that flood,*
> *Lose all their guilty stains.*[7]

Cowper's song led to the conversion of William Wilberforce, the English statesman most responsible for the abolition of slavery in Britain. Wilberforce was also an effective personal evangelist, winning Leigh Richmond, who later wrote a book, *The Dairyman's Daughter,* which was translated into 40 languages and advanced the cause of Christ worldwide.

All this, because of a mother's washboard prayers.[8]

I suggest that parents search the Scriptures for verses to pray into the lives of their children. Recently I found a passage I've claimed for my oldest daughter, Victoria. It's the priestly benediction recorded in Numbers 6:24-26. I "prayer-a-phrased" it in my devotional notebook to remind me to pray it into her character and life: "Dear Lord, bless Victoria and keep her; Make Your face to shine upon her and be gracious to her; Lift up Your countenance upon her, and give her peace."

We also rely on prayer for those moments in child-rearing that catch us unaware. Often, when faced with a decision or in a crisis, I've paused to pray silently, "Lord, show me what to do. Give me wisdom."

Our children stand tall and straight when we raise them on our knees.

Scripture Search: **Below is a "prayer-a-phrased" version of the Lord's Prayer (Matthew 6:9-15) written by a parent for her son, Thomas. In the margin, convert a passage of Scripture (this one or another) into a prayer for your child(ren).**

Our Father in heaven,
How holy is Your name.
May Your kingdom come,
Your will be done in Thomas' life
even as it is done in heaven.
Give him day by day his daily bread.
Meet all his needs. And forgive his sins,
helping him forgive those who sin against him.
Lead him not into temptation,
but deliver him from evil—and from the evil one.
And may he ascribe to you the kingdom, the power,
and the glory forever.
Amen.

A positive attitude. First Samuel 1 describes a third attitude that Hannah possessed. After patiently enduring the provocations of her rivals, and after prayerfully pouring out her soul to God, she "went her way and ate something, and her face was no longer downcast" (v. 18).

No lingering self-pity here! Hannah left her burdens before the Lord and chose to hold high her head with a smile on her face.

Biblical joy is more than positive thinking—but it isn't less! Happiness is an emotion, but joy and optimism are attitudes. Emotions come and go; but attitudes come and grow. Proverbs 15:15 claims, "The cheerful heart has a continual feast." Jesus amplified that truth in John

10:10: " 'I have come that they may have life, and have it to the full.' "

Through our relationship with Christ we can "take our burdens to the Lord and leave them there," a perfect description of Hannah's strategy. The writer of Hebrews echoed Jesus' words when he wrote: "For we do not have a high priest who is unable to sympathize with our weaknesses, but we have one who has been tempted in every way, just as we are—yet was without sin. Let us then approach the throne of grace with confidence, so that we may receive mercy and find grace to help us in our time of need" (Hebrews 4:15-16). When we come to Christ for His abundant life, when we bring our burdens to His throne, and when we claim His promises in prayer, we can then choose a cheerful heart.

And in so doing, we'll give our children a model of joy.

There's more to raising preschoolers than the right attitude, but we've got to start there. We need to be patient.

And prayerful.

And positive.

B = Bonding

First Samuel 1 goes on to say:

> So in the course of time Hannah conceived and gave birth to a son. She named him Samuel, saying, "Because I asked the Lord for him." When the man Elkanah went up with all his family to offer the annual sacrifice to the Lord and to fulfill his vow, Hannah did not go. She said to her husband, "After the boy is weaned, I will take him and present him before the Lord, and he will live there always."
>
> "Do what seems best to you," Elkanah her husband told her. "Stay here until you have weaned him; only may the Lord make good his word." So the woman stayed at home and nursed her son until she had weaned him (1 Samuel 1:20-23).

About the time my girls were born, a flurry of changes was occurring in maternity wards across the nation. Newborn babies had previously been tucked in little rolling carts, flown down the hall at blinding speeds, and isolated in sterile environments. They were only occasionally brought out by grudging nurses for mothers to feed.

When psychotherapists, studying animal traits, discovered that a specific bonding pattern is observable in practically all mammals, then gynecologists and pediatricians realized the importance of bonding between infant and mother. A revolution occurred in delivery rooms. Now the baby is typically deposited immediately from the womb into her parents' arms. She spends a lot of time in the hospital room with them, and ample opportunity is provided for initial bonding to occur.

Erik Erikson asserted that if you bond well with a loving, dependable parent during the first two years of life, you'll develop a reservoir of basic trust that you can draw from the rest of your life. But if you don't adequately bond with a loving parent or caregiver, you might deal with insecurity, anxiety, and sadness the rest of your life.[9]

The wording of 1 Samuel 1:23 is significant: "So the woman stayed at home and nursed her son."

To the extent that it's possible, babies need mothers to stay at home with them during the first critical months and years. Babies who don't adequately bond with their mothers may look the rest of their lives for the intimacy and security they missed during early childhood.

Admittedly, it isn't possible for all mothers to stay at home for extended periods with their babies. In some families, dads stay at home while moms work. Other families have grandparents or close friends who can help. In other cases, a high quality day-care program is necessary. Children may thrive in all these situations, but in every case they need rich, quality time with their parents, especially with mom.

That's one reason God gave mothers the ability to breast-feed their infants. Breast-feeding a child gives him a nutritional and medical head start in life, but it also provides an irreplaceable bonding between mother and child.

So Hannah stayed home and nursed her son until he was weaned.

 Let's Talk: **How can you bond with your child, given your particular schedule, demands, and circumstances? How do you feel about enrolling a baby in a day-care program? What creative ways have you found to satisfy your infant's need for intimacy with you?**

C = Consecration

At the right time, Elkanah and Hannah consecrated their son in the house of God (see 1 Samuel 1:24-28). Few books on parenting deal with this, but dedicating a child to the Lord is a dramatic and powerful moment. In our church, we invite parents to bring their babies to the altar and kneel at the front of our auditorium. They cradle their babies in their arms, and we pray for the children. We ask the Lord to bless and guide them all their days, and we dedicate them to God, like Hannah and Elkanah brought Samuel to the house of the Lord and dedicated him, and just as Mary and Joseph did with the infant Jesus in Jerusalem's temple.

In Luke 18, people were bringing their babies to Jesus to have Him touch and bless them. The disciples hindered the people, but Jesus rebuked them, " 'Let the little children come to me, and do not hinder them' " (v. 16). When you give your most precious possession, your children, to the Lord, He'll bless them and use them in ways far greater than you'll ever design or imagine.

Two generations of Christians have been moved by the story of John and Betty Stam, missionaries to China. They went to China in the 1930s, were married there, and gave birth to a daughter, Helen Priscilla. One Sunday in 1934, they took their little girl to a Chinese church. The pastor took the baby in his arms, dedicated her to the Lord, prayed that she might grow up like the Priscilla in the New Testament, and entrusted her to the Lord.

A few days later, Communist forces stormed into their house, bound John and carried him off, then returned for Betty and the baby who was only three months old. The soldiers told the Stams that as part of their torture, they would be forced to witness their baby's death. Suddenly a stranger came from nowhere and begged them to spare the child. The soldier said, "Then it's your life for hers!" The man replied, "I am willing," and he was shot on the spot.

The little family was marched to another city and imprisoned in a private home. The next morning, John and Betty were led out to be killed by sword. The baby was left behind in the deserted house.

All day, the little three-month-old orphan lay there, and all night she cried in the darkness. No one answered.

But that child belonged to the Lord. A national Chinese evangelist came into the village. He heard whispers about a foreigner's baby abandoned in a prison house. He crept into the house and found the baby zipped up in her sleeping bag just as her mother had left her 30 hours before. Miraculously, Helen Priscilla was smuggled to safety. Her escape required several months and involved countless miracles, but the Lord moved heaven and earth to safeguard that little girl who, only days before, had been entrusted to His will.

You'll never go wrong in giving your children to God. Share with Him the burdens and responsibilities of raising them.

D = Dad

The spiritual devotion of Elkanah is impressive, for he lived in a land where everyone did what was right in their own eyes, and few did what was right in the eyes of God. Yet, "Year after year this man went up from his town to worship and sacrifice to the Lord Almighty at Shiloh" (see 1 Samuel 1:3 and 2:18). He also led his family to worship (see also 1 Samuel 1:21).

Three times we're told that Elkanah was a man who made his unashamed vow to the Lord, worshiped regularly, and led his family spiritually. It's no wonder that we're also told, "And the boy Samuel continued to grow in stature and in favor with the Lord and with men" (1 Samuel 2:26).

Every child needs a father like that who loves the Lord and leads his family in worship. Happy are toddlers whose fathers still them long enough for prayer. Fortunate are children whose dads go with them to church Sunday by Sunday.

Fathers also affect the emotional climate at home. If Dad's calm, warm, affectionate, and demonstrative, his home will be stable. If he's volatile, distant, severe, or weak, his home will become a damaging environment. And a weak, passive dad coupled with a strong, vocal, domineering mother opens a Pandora's box of problems for children.

Some of my happiest moments came when my girls were very young. I'd rock them to sleep at night, softly singing spontaneous medleys of my favorite hymns. I'd almost become teary-eyed as I looked down at my little girls and sang about how God loves them and me.

Scripture Search: **Read the verses below giving the example of God's fatherhood. Complete the sentence beneath each one using one of the following words:**

gifts, needs, respect, loves, fellowship, discipline, commends, welfare, compassionate

Our fellowship is with the Father and with his Son, Jesus Christ (1 John 1:3).
A good father should enjoy _____ with his children.

How great is the love the Father has lavished on us, that we should be called children of God (1 John 3:1).
A good father _____ his children lavishly.

Your father knows what you need before you ask him (Matthew 6:8, see also Matthew 7:9-11).
A good father is sensitive to his children's _____.

As a father has compassion on his children,
*   so the Lord has compassion on those who fear him*
*   (Psalm 103:13).*
A good father is _____.

It has given me great joy to find some of your children walking in the truth just as the Father commanded us (2 John 4).
A good father gives his children wise _____.

"In the same way your Father in heaven is not willing that any of these little ones should be lost" (Matthew 18:14).
A good father is concerned about his children's spiritual _____.

Endure hardship as discipline; God is treating you as sons. For what son is not disciplined by his father? (Hebrews 12:7).
A good father provides loving but firm _____ .

Every good and perfect gift is from above, coming down from the Father of the heavenly lights (James 1:17).
A good father enjoys surprising his children with good _____.

E = Environment

Psychologists have a lot to say about children's environment, but they'll never find a healthier environment than Samuel's.

But Samuel was ministering before the Lord—a boy wearing a linen ephod. Each year his mother made him a little robe and took it to him when she went up with her husband to offer the annual sacrifice. Eli would bless Elkanah and his wife, saying, "May the Lord give you children by this woman to take the place of the one she prayed for and gave to the Lord." Then they would go home. And the Lord was gracious to Hannah; she conceived and gave birth to three sons and two daughters. Meanwhile, the boy Samuel grew up in the presence of the Lord (1 Samuel 2:18-21).

Today we would say Samuel grew up in church. My parents took me to church from my infancy. I attended Sunday worship services my first Lord's Day on earth. The first Bible verse I remember memorizing was one I learned in Sunday School—Psalm 122:1: "I was glad when they said unto me, Let us go into the house of the Lord" (KJV).

"The local church you choose for your children to grow up in will become one of the major influences on their self-concepts," writes Paul Meier. "If you're in a negativistic, legalistic church that neglects God's grace, you're in the wrong boat! ... Or if you are in a liberal church, supposing it to be a sinking ship you can save, your children will probably sink with it. I would recommend that you get your family into a church where the Bible is accepted as the errorless Word of God, where souls are being saved, where genuine Christian love is practiced."[10]

 Let's Talk: **As a parent, what do you look for in your church?**

I'm bothered that many parents consider church attendance a convenience-based option. They bring their families to church if the weather's nice, if no one is sick, and if there's nothing else to do. If I'd grown up that way, my church involvement would have fluctuated widely. Vance Havner once said this of his father who took him to church:

Whether the weather be good
Or whether the weather be hot,
Whether the weather be cold
Or whether the weather be not,
Whatever the weather, he weathered the weather,
Whether he liked it or not.[11]

What does it take to raise preschoolers?

It takes a dad and mom who know the ABCs of raising kids, and who are willing to say, as Joshua said long ago: " 'As for me and my household, we will serve the Lord' " (Joshua 24:15).

P.S. (Practical Suggestions from Chapter 6)

1. If you're a new mother, consider the possibilities and consequences of remaining home with your baby for an extended period.

2. If you must place your young child in a day-care program, find one that is Christian in its orientation; clean; and staffed by gentle, well-trained, Christian workers with a low worker/child ratio.

3. Talk with your pastor about your church's traditions for dedicating children. Schedule a time to publicly dedicate your child to Christ.

4. Take your child to church regularly as soon as possible after birth. If you aren't presently attending church, look for one with a well-designed children's program.

5. To develop a more patient attitude, discuss with your spouse or a friend ways you can successfully implement the five steps to a patient attitude. Copy Proverbs 16:32, Proverbs 29:11, Galatians 5:22, Ephesians 4:2, and Ephesians 4:26-27 word-for-word on adhesive-backed notes, placing them where you will see them often. Even better, read the last 20 chapters of Proverbs and find your own verses to memorize! If, despite your best efforts, you can't bring your anger under control, consult your minister and doctor for help.

6. To develop a more prayerful attitude, pray aloud for your child by name one full minute each day. Day-by-day, increase the allotment of time you pray for your child.

7. To develop a more positive attitude, spend time in prayer, confessing your lack of joy and gladness to the Lord. Ask Him for help. Then:
   - Read Psalm 103 aloud once a day.
   - Tune your radio to uplifting Christian music.
   - Begin an exercise program.
   - As a family project, memorize Proverbs 15:15 or John 10:10.
   - Before you fall asleep at night repeat Isaiah 40:31.

[1]Theodore Lidz, *The Person* (New York: Basic Books, 1968), 117.
[2]Paul D. Meier, *Christian Child-Rearing and Personality Development* (Grand Rapids: Baker Book House, 1977), ix.
[3]Nancy Samalin, *Love and Anger, the Parental Dilemma* (New York: Penguin Books, 1991), 5.
[4]Melvin Konner, *Childhood* (Boston: Little, Brown, and Company), 69.
[5]Clint Bonner, *A Hymn Is Born* (Nashville: Broadman, 1959), 16.
[6]John Newton, "Amazing Grace! How Sweet the Sound," *The Baptist Hymnal,* © Copyright 1991, Convention Press. All rights reserved. International copyright secured. Used by permission.
[7]William Cowper, "There Is a Fountain," *The Baptist Hymnal,* Convention Press. All rights reserved. International copyright secured. Used by permission.
[8]Mrs. Charles E. Cowman, *Springs in the Valley* (Los Angeles: Cowman Publications, Inc., 1939), 241.
[9]Konner, *Childhood*, 90.
[10]Meier, *Christian Child-Rearing*, 13.
[11]Vance Havner, *Salt and Pepper* (Old Tappan, N.J.: Fleming H. Revell Company, 1966), 26.

~ 7 ~
Raising Confident Elementary-Age Kids

How do you like to go up in a swing,
Up in the air so blue?
Oh, I do think it the pleasantest thing
Ever a child can do![1]

Those words from Robert Louis Stevenson's *A Child's Garden of Verses* typify the elementary years—or middle childhood, in psychological jargon—as comparatively calm for many kids. Youngsters don't grow as quickly during middle childhood as they did during the preschool years or as they will during adolescence. One textbook suggests that the ages 7 to 11 are the best years of the entire life span, relatively smooth and uneventful for several reasons:

> *For one, disease and death are rarer during these years than during any other period. For another, most children master new physical skills without much adult instruction. ... In addition, sex differences in physical development and ability are minimal, and sexual urges seem to be submerged. Certainly, when physical development during these years is compared with the rapid and dramatic changes that occur during adolescence, middle childhood seems a period of relative tranquillity.*[2]

But one area of child development has increasingly emerged as a mine field during this span of life: self-image. A child ought to leap out of these years more confident, thankful, and optimistic than ever. But increasingly, children are leaving middle childhood with self-images damaged by the nature of our educational systems, our athletic preoccupation, the energy of peer pressure, the insensitivity of parents, and media perceptions pushed on them. All these unwittingly join forces to slowly erode a child's self-image. A primary task of empowered parents is helping our youngsters develop self-confidence and a healthy self-image during middle childhood.

The Word of God is a double-edged sword, and Romans 12:3 certainly has two edges in addressing this issue: "Do not think of yourself more highly than you ought, but rather think of yourself with sober judgment, in accordance with the measure of faith God has given you."

The words *do not think of yourself more highly than you ought* contain two implications. First, we aren't to think of ourselves too highly; we shouldn't be proud through an inflated self-concept. But the wording also suggests we shouldn't think too poorly of ourselves either. Paul *didn't* say, "Don't think of yourself highly." He told us to think of ourselves realistically as one lovingly created in God's image, yet without self-centeredness for we are all sinners needing His redemptive touch.

 ***Let's Talk:* Was your self-image built up or eroded during your elementary years? Why?**

What then can parents do to raise optimistic and confident children during the elementary years? The best advice is found in Ephesians 6:4, "Fathers, do not exasperate your children; instead, bring them up in the training and instruction of the Lord."

The Living Bible puts it: "And now a word to you parents. Don't keep on scolding and nagging your children, making them angry and resentful. Rather, bring them up with the loving discipline the Lord himself approves, with suggestions and godly advice."

How do we do that? Let me share with you five vital code words.

Respect

Sometimes parents think of themselves as drill sergeants instead of divine stewards. Our children don't belong to us like raw recruits; they are entrusted to us as treasures, and we treat our treasures with respect. Show children common courtesy and good manners. That doesn't mean we don't give direction or require obedience; but it does mean that we build up our children's self-esteem by letting them know we respect them as treasures from the Lord.

A child draws his self-portrait with colors borrowed from his parents' palette. The greatest influence on his self-concept is his perception of how much those most important to him esteem him. If he feels respected by his parents, he'll develop respect for himself.

I'm not an expert father, but I'd like to recommend some of the courtesies I've tried to extend to my children.

I've tried never to discipline or correct my kids in public or in front of their friends, or even in front of their siblings. Humiliation is never an acceptable tool of discipline.

I've tried never to walk into their rooms without knocking first and asking permission. Children won't develop a good self-image if they don't have sufficient time alone to get to know themselves. Right now my 10-year-old has a sign taped to her bedroom door. It reads:

You have come to Grace's room

Rules

1. *Knock.*
2. *Do not walk in unless I say you can.*
3. *If I am not in my room, leave; do not come in and take anything you want unless you have permission (from me).*
4. *Don't keep knocking while I come to unlock the door.*
5. *Don't kick or abuse my door.*
6. *If I say, "Go away," do so. If I say, "I don't want to talk right now," leave.*

I think those are pretty good rules, and I'm considering posting them on my office door. Although many children don't have the privilege of a bedroom all their own, all children find their own special places; and all children need places of solitude to develop their friendship with their own hearts.

Besides, I don't want them barging through my closed bedroom door without knocking. Shouldn't I treat them as I expect to be treated?

Scripture Search: **Look up the following "one another" verses and fill in the blanks. Since our children are included in the "one another" category, I've applied the verses to our behavior toward them.**

Romans 12:10 - Be _____ to your children in brotherly love.

Romans 12:10 - _____ your children above yourselves.

Romans 12:16 - Live in _____ with your children.

Galatians 5:13 - _____ your children in love.

Ephesians 4:32 - Be _____ and _____ to your children, forgiving them.

Colossians 3:16 - _____ and _____ your children with all wisdom.

1 Thessalonians 5:11 - _____ your children and build them up.

1 Peter 1:22 - _____ your children deeply from your heart.

Circle the three statements describing areas where you most need growth as a parent.

I've never pried through my children's private papers or read their correspondence. They know they can write anything in their diaries and leave them anywhere in the house, and I'll never violate their trust by reading them.

Similarly, I've tried never to betray their confidence. I don't even tell my wife the things they confide to me. And she doesn't let me in on their private conversations with her.

I've tried never to say no to their requests without explaining why. In fact, I may have overdone it. Recently one of my daughters asked for something, and I started a long, rambling explanation as to why I didn't think it best. She interrupted me, saying, "Dad, it's all right to say no; you don't have to spend ten minutes telling me why." Well, I'd rather they'd have that attitude than be frustrated by rules without reasons and denials without explanations.

I've tried never to kid them in a demeaning or a sarcastic way. We do joke with each other, and sometimes laugh at one another; but never with sarcasm, ridicule, put-downs, or cutting remarks. Children raised with sarcasm, become sarcastic adults and I feel sorry for the persons they marry. Much of the so-called humor on television is sarcasm; and we should refuse to watch it. Otherwise, it seeps into our homes and creeps into our conversations without our realizing it.

I've tried to treat my daughters' friends with respect, and they are welcome at our house. In fact, I'd rather have my daughters and their friends at our house where we have some control over the standards of language and conduct than to have our children at another house where we may not know what is acceptable.

I've tried never to be too busy for them. At times I've had to say, "I can't take time right now." But I try to become available just as soon as possible. I want them to know they're more important to me than all the other people I deal with put together.

I never expect my children to act any differently because I am a pastor. If they're forbidden to do something, it's because we're a Christian family, not because we're a pastoral family.

And I've always tried to apologize when I've been wrong. My wife Katrina told me the other day: "I've made so many mistakes in raising the children, but at least I've apologized when I've lost my temper or acted inappropriately. That's why I think we still have an open and happy relationship."

Those are some of my own personal rules for raising children based on the premise that if we treat them with respect, they'll learn to respect themselves. They'll grow up to be respectable adults, and to treat us with respect when they (and we) are older.

Discipline

Discipline—that's really the thrust of Ephesians 6:4, for both the words *nurture* and *instruction* in the Greek convey the idea of discipline. Chapter 9 deals exclusively with this, but for now, observe the link between discipline and a child's self-image.

When you are undisciplined—going on an eating or spending binge for example—how does that make you think of yourself? When you overreact or lose your temper, does it enhance your self-image? Usually, an undisciplined person doesn't feel good about himself.

When recovering alcoholics relapse, the battering it gives their self-image is heartbreaking. They feel like dirt.

Children's self-assurance grows in equal proportion to their self-discipline. Since self-discipline is a learned habit, wise moderate parental discipline is required up front.

***Let's Talk:* Do you see how self-discipline is related to self-image in your life? What can you do to bolster your children's self-discipline?**

Encourage

Children need massive doses of encouragement. Zig Ziglar tells of a study that divided 60 school children into three groups of 20 who were given arithmetic tests daily for five days. One group was consistently praised for its previous performance; another group was criticized; the third was ignored. Those who were praised improved dramatically; those who were criticized improved also, but not as much; and those who were ignored hardly improved at all.[4]

Ziglar said, "Children who are raised in a spirit of praise and approval are going to be happier, more productive, and more obedient than the ones who are constantly criticized."[5]

During college, I worked in several Billy Graham crusades and heard Cliff Barrows tell about his first lesson in leading music. While quite young, he was asked to lead worship at his church. The people didn't sing very well, so he scolded them, saying, "This is the worst singing I've ever heard. I'm ashamed of you. Now, come on and do better."

Returning home, his father told him something he never forgot. "Cliff," he said, "you'll never get people to sing better by scolding them and telling them how badly they're doing. You have to tell them that they're doing pretty well, and that you think they can do a little better."

Many times I've followed that advice, for encouragement is fertilizer to a child's growing self-identity.

Teach

Specifically, we need to teach them to know God. Chapter 13 addresses this, but for now, let me offer two suggestions.

First, we must provide our children with a theological basis for a healthy self-image. Our society says, "You're valuable and important because you're handsome or beautiful; because you excel at basketball, baseball, or soccer; because you make terrific grades; because your folks have a lot of money; because you wear trendy clothes."

The Bible says we're valuable and important because God made us in His image and He loves us so much that His Son died for our benefit.

Through the years, we've told our girls that "pretty" isn't important. We've taught them to stay in shape, take care of themselves, be attractive and presentable, but not to place worldly value on outward appearance. The Bible says genuine attractiveness is not a matter of outward appearance, but of inward beauty. Imagine the ramifications on a girl's emerging self-image—the freedom and joy it would give her— to memorize Proverbs 31:30: "Charm is deceptive, and beauty is fleeting; but a woman who fears the Lord is to be praised." Boys can learn the verse spoken about young David and his brothers: "Pay no attention to how tall and handsome he is. ... I do not judge as man judges. Man looks at the outward appearance, but I look at the heart" (1 Samuel 16:7, GNB).

Second, we need to teach our children to delve into the Bible and discover verses for themselves. When our girls were younger, the family altar was rather brief. We'd read a short portion of Scripture or from an appropriate devotional book, then offer a one-minute prayer.

Now that my daughters are older, I'm more concerned that they have devotions on their own. I want them to enter adulthood walking with God through the practice of a daily quiet time.

I've purchased an appropriate Bible for each of my daughters, and even notebooks and journals. Each evening we ask them to spend time in Bible reading and prayer, meeting with their Master in the quietness of bedtime. When the Creator of the universe asks to spend time with us each day, it can only bolster our confidence in living life.

Our self-concepts should never be deeper than our God-concept. Our faith in ourselves should never be greater than our faith in God. No one is more confident in life than the person who knows the Lord Jesus, who is walking with Him, and who lives in His perfect will.

 Let's Talk: **What techniques have worked for you in (a) personal devotions; and (b) helping your children develop devotional habits of their own?**

Love

The year that Hannah, my middle daughter, was born, Dr. Ross Campbell, a Chattanooga psychologist, authored a book called *How to Really Love Your Child.* That book had a deep effect on my parenting. Dr. Campbell's thesis is that most parents really do love their children, but many of them don't convey that love to a child in a way that really makes that child feel secure.[6] A child doesn't just need to be loved, he needs to feel loved. And many of them don't.

There are several ways to convey love to children. We can, of course, tell them we love them. The simple words "I love you" are powerful!

But we can convey love also through our eyes. We often use our eyes to convey disapproval and discipline, but the laughter of love in a parent's eye says more to a child than a dozen "I love you's."

We also convey love to children by the amount of time we spend with them. My dad occasionally set aside an entire day to do with me whatever I wanted. I've tried to follow his example by planning regular "dates" with my girls, taking them out to dinner at their favorite restaurant (we finally outgrew McDonald's), and on various outings. Occasionally I will take them, one at a time, on business trips with me, especially if we can squeeze in a day at a nearby theme park or beach. Your children will measure your love for them chiefly by the amount of time you invest in their company.

And we convey love physically, by touching, holding, rough-housing, and embracing. I'm a great believer in "hug therapy." The other day I hugged one of my girls and I think it embarrassed her, for I overheard her tell her friend, "My dad hugs a lot. It's just something I've had to learn to live with."

Let's Talk: **Discuss in a group setting ways in which you felt parental love (or the lack of it) during your own childhood.**

 ***Scripture Search:*** **Finish the sentences using the 15 qualities of love given in 1 Corinthians 13:4-8.**

Love is patient, love is kind. It does not envy, it does not boast, it is not proud. It is not rude, it is not self-seeking, it is not easily angered, it keeps no record of wrongs. Love does not delight in evil but rejoices with the truth. It always protects, always trusts, always hopes, always perseveres. Love never fails.

A loving parent ...
is _____;
is _____;
does not _____;
does not _____;
is not _____;
is not _____;
is not _____;
keeps _____;
does not _____;
rejoices with _____;
always _____;
always _____;
always _____;
always _____.
This kind of parental love never _____.

Our kids require respect, discipline, encouragement, sound teaching, and love during the foundational years of childhood. We're living in a broken society filled with people who don't like themselves. Those who remove the Word of God from the foundation of society, replacing it with a theory that we just emerged from a glob of evolutionary sludge, destroy the basis for human self-esteem. But Christian parents, armed with the infallible Scriptures, can still raise confident, strong, optimistic, self-assured children if they know the code words. So, "Fathers [and mothers], do not exasperate your children; instead, bring them up in the training and instruction of the Lord" (Ephesians 6:4).

P.S. (Practical Suggestions from Chapter 7)

1. Guide your child to choose "alone time" each day, an opportunity to enjoy being alone for a few minutes. Suggest your child play quietly, or thumb through picture books, or take a nap. While the television should remain off during this time, some soft Christian music might be appropriate.

2. Listen to yourself as you speak to your spouse and/or children. Begin weeding out negative, cutting, sarcastic words.

3. Read Zig Ziglar's *Raising Positive Kids in a Negative World,* and Dr. Ross Campbell's *How to Really Love Your Child.* Ask your church or one near you to offer a study of *Parenting by Grace.*[7]

4. Begin family devotions. Make them brief, Bible-centered times of reading Scripture and prayer. Many devotional books are published for families with children of all ages. *The Family Worship Bible* published by Broadman and Holman provides all you need for family worship in one volume.

6. Become a student of creationism, and share with your child the insights you learn about the creating genius of God.

7. Plan a date with your child.

---

[1] Robert Louis Stevenson, *A Child's Garden of Verses* (New York: Franklin Watts, Inc., 1966), 17.
[2] Berger, *The Developing Person Through the Life Span,* 247.
[3] Ibid., 249.
[4] Ziglar, *Raising Positive Kids in a Negative World,* 52-53.
[5] Ibid., 53.
[6] D. Ross Campbell, *How to Really Love Your Child* (Wheaton: Victor Books, 1980).
[7] To order *Parenting by Grace* resources, call 1-800-458-2772, or vist your local Baptist Bookstore or Lifeway Christian Store.

~ 8 ~
The Joy of Raising Teenagers

Several years ago on a flight from Brazil to Miami, the captain told us to fasten our seat belts and prepare for turbulence. Radar showed a hurricane over the Caribbean. I secured my seat belt and nodded off, only to be jolted awake. Our plane shuddered and jerked as though drunk, and the wind tossed us around like tissue. We prayed and clung to our seats for dear life.

Over the years people have spoken to me about parenting like our captain warned of the hurricane. "Your children are young, and everything's calm. But fasten your seat belts! The teen years are coming; there's turbulence ahead."

That's been the psychological view for decades. The word *adolescence* was coined by the founder of American developmental psychology, G. Stanley Hall, from a Latin word meaning *growth*. Hall argued that the erratic physical growth of adolescents coincides with volatile emotional and moral development; and "every step of the upward way is strewn with wreckage of body, mind, and morals."[1]

Many psychologists feel that "the stresses of adolescence are inescapable, since the adolescent's rapid sexual maturation and powerful sexual drives inevitably conflict with the culture's traditional prohibitions against their free expression and their parents' reluctance to accept the maturation of their children."[2]

Turbulence

Adolescent alienation is a major problem in our society, and millions of teenagers are at risk. A recent report found that 1 in 7 teens has attempted suicide. Fifty-six percent of girls and 35 percent of boys claim it's hard to cope with stresses at home and school, and 34 percent of girls and 15 percent of boys say they often feel sad and hopeless.[3]

Another study showed that the following 10 problems, in order, plague teenagers today more than any other time: drug abuse, alcohol abuse, negative peer pressure, unwanted pregnancy, child abuse, teen crime, depression, conflict with parents, suicide, and runaway behavior.

"There's less structure for teens today, what with working mothers, single parents, the availability of drugs and the impersonal nature of modern life," writes Dr. John Meeks, a medical director in Maryland.[4]

But ...

But that's not the whole story. I've flown many times across the nation and around the world. All flights have some vibration, and some encounter a little turbulence. But most flights are relatively calm. Severe turbulence is the exception, and I don't board airplanes automatically expecting it.

Nor did I enter the second decade of parenthood expecting it. Several recent studies are now actually reporting that the teen years are often among the richest for parent-child relationships. "Careful research on large samples of young people over the past two decades has led to the conclusion that most adolescents, most of the time, are calm, predictable and purposeful rather than storm-tossed, erratic, and 'lost.' "[5]

Zipora Magen of the University of Tel Aviv concluded from her study on parent-teen relationships that adolescents appreciate parental authority and guidance more than they let on. "Generally, parents and their adolescent offspring have similar perceptions of what makes a good parent. It's just that parents and teens think there are bigger differences between them than there really are. Each side tends to underestimate the positive attitude held toward them by the other side."[6]

USA Today printed a story under the headline, "Teens to Parents: You're OK." The newspaper reported that 75 percent of 584 youth, aged 11 to 16, felt very close to both parents. Penn State sociologist Kathleen Harris said that recent research belies the "popular assumption that adolescence is a rocky time for parents and kids."[7]

According to a Gallup Youth Survey, teenagers are just as likely as adults to believe in God, but more likely to attend church.[8]

Many teenagers in the Bible were already heroes in God's eyes. Joseph retained a tender friendship with his father Jacob. David, Jesse's youngest son, was secretly anointed king of Israel while still at home watching his father's flocks. Daniel and his three friends were pressed into Babylonian service, apparently as teenagers. And there was another God-fearing, synagogue-attending youth whose teen years are summarized in one New Testament verse: "And Jesus grew in wisdom and stature, and in favor with God and men" (Luke 2:52).

In other words, Jesus' teen years were marked by spurts of growth typical of adolescence. He grew intellectually, physically, socially, and spiritually.

How can we raise teenagers like that?

By *horizontalizing*.

 ***Let's Talk:* Recall your own teen years. What were your biggest struggles? How did you relate to your parents?**

Horizontalizing

When our children are born, we find ourselves in an almost totally vertical relationship with them. They're absolutely dependent on us, and we possess total responsibility over their lives.

But as our kids grow older the vertical line begins to shift a few degrees; and the older they become, the more our relationship with them horizontalizes. We become less and less authority figures, and more and more friends. Remember, as long as we're able, we'll bear certain responsibilities for our children and expect their loving respect. In fact, as we age the horizontal line often begins to verticalize again, with our kids assuming care and responsibility for us.

But during our children's adolescent years we gradually exchange authority over them for fellowship with them. How can we provide a supportive environment that moves our teens toward autonomy and independence? Gradually horizontalizing our relationship with our children involves several simultaneous stages.

1. We move from controller to companion. First, horizontalizing means that we gradually move from controller to companion. We become their peers as well as their parents.

We don't suddenly abdicate our authority as parents; we still make decisions, set curfews, and require accountability. But we do it less unilaterally. We allow our teens to participate in decision-making, and increasingly allow them to shape the decisions that affect their lives. We say yes whenever we can, and no when we must; and when we do say no, we provide an adequate explanation.

We begin enjoying a more mature relationship. I used to become sentimental and sad when I noticed how quickly my daughters were growing up. I'd ask myself, "Why can't they stay this young and sweet always?" But one day I determined I wasn't going to be sentimental about it any longer. Every age is better than the previous one; every stage is advancement. As my daughters mature, so does our friendship; it just gets better and better.

Jay Kesler says in his book, *Ten Mistakes Parents Make with Teenagers*:

> *Adolescence is not something to be dreaded or survived. My wife, Janie, and I have raised our children and are now enjoying our six grandchildren. Yet we would both say that the teenage years were our most enjoyable years of child raising, for it was then we traded portability for compatibility. ...*
>
> *We edge into an adult-to-adult relationship with them, sharing ideas, dreams, opinions, and experiences.*[9]

Scrípture Search: **Proverbs seems to be composed of wise sayings from a father to his teenage son. Read the following verses, consider their relevance to raising teens, and complete the sentences below the verses.**

A fool shows his annoyance at once,
  but a prudent man overlooks an insult (Proverbs 12:16).
A man's wisdom gives him patience;
  it is to his glory to overlook an offense (Proverbs 19:11).
The thing I frequently have to "overlook" with my teen is ...

_____

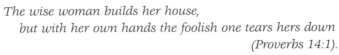

The wise woman builds her house,
but with her own hands the foolish one tears hers down
(Proverbs 14:1).
The best ways I've found for building up my teen are ...

_____

A heart of the righteous weighs its answers (Proverbs 15:28).
I need the most wisdom when talking to my teen about ...

_____

The purposes of a man's heart are deep waters,
but a man of understanding draws them out
(Proverbs 20:5).
I've been most successful in drawing my teen out when we ...

_____

2. We move from talking to listening. When our children are young, we do a lot of talking. We instruct, syllogize, teach, lecture, harangue, rant, rave, and nag. But teenagers won't put up with much of that.

They tend to resent the mildest suggestions. That means we should move from microphone to earphone. I'm not suggesting we never advise or counsel. Sometimes we need to rant, rave, and nag a little!

But primarily we have to listen, for teens value parents' ears more than their mouths. When our children are younger, we do most of the talking; as they grow older, we do most of the listening. That, after all, is a mark of maturity: "Everyone should be quick to listen, slow to speak and slow to become angry" (James 1:19).

 Let's Talk: **Why is it so difficult for us parents to listen to our teens without offering advice prematurely or excessively?**

I've learned slowly. By profession, I'm a communicator—a writer, a public speaker. I'm supposed to be good at it, and I get paid for it. But in practice, I struggle to communicate with my kids just like you do. It's easy to jabber for an hour into a microphone before a roomful of nodding listeners—even if they're nodding for different reasons. But drawing my adolescent kid into a ponderous conversation ... well, that's another matter. Teens don't open up easily. The changes occurring in their lives make them feel vulnerable. Their egos are fragile. Their feelings are tangled.

The result? Their communications apparatus shuts down. They sit at the dinner table and establish eye contact only with their chicken.

They retreat to their rooms, shut the door, and remain *incommunicado*. They spend hours on the phone, talking to friends who are less threatening than parents, but only seconds talking to parents who are presumably more loving than friends.

Parent-teen conversations often resemble inquests. We employ questions like crowbars to pry lose little bits of data, and they respond with name, rank, and serial number.

The other day, for example, as I drove my 13-year-old to piano practice, we somehow managed to squeeze the following conversation into the 15-minute trip:

"Hannah?"

"Huh?"

"How was your day?"

"OK."

"Well, did you have any tests?"

"No."

"Well, did anything unusual happen? Any assembly programs? Any ball games? Any fights in the hallways?"

"No, Dad. It was a normal day."

(Pause)

"Were all your friends at school today?"

"Yeah."

"Well, did you get any grades back?"

"No, Dad. (Pause) You sure ask a lot of questions."

"Well, that's because I'm interested in you; and I'm interested in the things that happened to you today."

"Well, nothing happened today."

(Pause)

"Do you have any homework?"

"A little. But I can get it done before bedtime."

"Do you need any help?"

"Nope."

"I hope you have a good piano lesson."

"Thanks, Dad."

While she had her piano lesson, I ordered a cup of coffee at McDonald's and scratched my head. A half-hour later I pulled curbside, and Hannah bounded out of the house and hopped in the car. I was late for an appointment, so I was focused on getting home ASAP.

As I maneuvered through the traffic, Hannah said, "By the way, Dad, did I tell you about the dog that had a problem with gas?"

"The dog that what?"

"The dog that passed gas."

"No, I don't think you did, but I wish that truck would move!"

"It was a boxer named Cedric."

"Hannah, I'm going to be late for my appointment!"

"Well you see, Dad, he was a beautiful dog, but you couldn't stay in the same room with him because ..."

"Good grief! The light's gonna catch me."

"... because every minute or two a terrible odor would fill the room. The lady who owned him tried everything to solve his problem, but it just got worse. Sometimes he'd make a bad sound, and other times you just smelled it."

"I don't like this story, Hannah. Where did you hear it?"

"I read it last night in the James Herriot book of dog stories you gave me for Christmas."

"Oh."

"Well, Cedric's owner called Dr. Herriot, but he couldn't do anything. She didn't want to put her dog to sleep, but no one could stand to be around him. I mean, he had a constant exhaust."

"We're only seven minutes from home; get ready to jump out."

"It was a real problem, dad. The lady who owned him had to live with a handkerchief over her nose."

"My, my. Do you have your piano books in your hand?"

"But there was a neighbor who liked Cedric and kept him while his owner went on trips. Cedric's owner decided she just couldn't live with his vapors any longer, and she gave him to this man. Everyone wondered how the man could bear to live in the same house with Cedric."

"I hate being late."

"Well, one day Dr. Herriot came by to visit. He no sooner walked in the room than a overpowering odor rose from the dog. He saw a vase of flowers nearby. He stuck his nose in them, and breathed deeply, and pretended to admire them. 'Oh yes,' said the man. 'A friend gave them to me. But I don't get the full benefit from them.' Dr. Herriot asked what he meant. 'I had an operation for adenoids when I was a kid,' said the man, 'and something went wrong. I have no sense of smell.' "

At that, Hannah erupted into chortling. At the same moment, I pulled into our driveway and prepared to push her from the car. And then I realized ...

I realized that Hannah had just let me into her inner world; she had communicated with me. She had told me what had captivated her attention last night. She had told me what she had been talking about with her friends that morning. She had told me the little story that had brought a grin to her lips throughout her day at school.

She had told me all that, and I had almost missed it.

I touched her arm as she started out the door. "You say his name was Cedric?" I asked. She turned, our eyes met, we laughed, and for the first time that evening, we committed first-degree communication.

I learned a couple of things that night. First, if I expect my kids to tell me what I want to know, I need to listen to what they want to say.

Second, I need to capitalize on those communicative moments. We won't connect using Twenty Questions; we have to catch those spontaneous times when the barriers are down.

3. *We move from spending time with them to spending more time with them.* Parents often feel that as their children enter adolescence, the time burdens of parenting lessen. Teenagers grow increasingly independent and seem to enjoy the company of buddies more than "quality family time." So parents naturally assume they can use this free time for their own purposes and leisure.

Wrong.

Teens need more, not less, of their parents' time. How do you create "positive family attachments" with your teen? Where do you find "prime time" with your busy adolescent? Here are some suggestions.

Tea Time. You can't believe I suggested that, can you? I know it sounds hopelessly Victorian, but through the years my wife has fixed hot tea and cakes for the girls when they arrived home from school. It was a smart move, for often the conversation flowed faster than the tea. Often on Fridays, I'll pick up one of my teens at school and drive to a little cafe where I'll order coffee, she'll order tea, and we'll talk.

Meal Time. In many homes, meals are the only time the whole family is together in one place at one time. Society demands a lot from us, and our schedules reflect the pressures that pull us apart. Pressure to eat in shifts, pressure to skip meals, pressure to grab a bite on the run. Fight back! Insist on some family suppers. What better time to chew the fat? The family that chows together chats together!

Post-Trauma Time. After a teen suffers emotional upset, they may want to talk. I know a dad whose 13-year-old daughter, Ruth, has a Great Dane that recently ran away. When she yelled to him, he looked back as if saying, "Bet you can't catch me!" He then turned and romped off to terrify the neighbors. Ruth, furious, sat in the living room window waiting for him to return. Wisps of smoke curled out of her ears.

When Bismark finally dragged himself home, Ruth's wrath knew no bounds, and the Dane got what was coming to him. My friend walked in just as she stormed to her room, still trembling with rage. Her door slammed, then a couple of objects crashed against the wall.

He waited about 20 minutes then knocked on her door.

As he expected, a wave of depression had followed her spent fury. She looked at the floor and choked back tears. "What's wrong with me, Daddy?" she cried. "Why do I get so mad?"

My friend held his daughter in his arms awhile and they talked about anger. Then he helped her repair the ceramic she had broken. It was a rare moment of openness.

The teen years are mine fields of stress, so lend an understanding ear at those just-the-right times.

Down Time. The best communicative moments of all, of course, are the down times. Trips, hikes, leisure activities, hobbies, sitting around a camp fire or in a garden swing—those relaxed moments when teens unwind, lower their defenses, and conversation seems natural.

Find out what your youngsters like to do, and do it with them. Is it shopping? Find a sale. Is it an amusement park? Ride a roller coaster together. Is it the great outdoors? Buy a couple of sleeping bags. Is it a hamburger and shake? Try out some new restaurants.

Bed Time. Finally, learn to take advantage of bed time. Children never grow too old to tuck-in, one way or another. Bedsides were made for parents to sit on, and with the lights low and the day done, teenagers often feel a coziness that allows them to share some of their precious, private thoughts. A sensitive parent just listens, reassures, hugs, and treasures the moment.

I read of a lady whose teenage daughter had a separate phone line. She'd come home from school, grunt to her mom, and disappear into her room where she'd spend hours talking to her friends on the phone. Finally, the mother seized on an idea. At bedtime, she would prop herself on her pillow, call upstairs, and chat with her phone-loving daughter. The two of them chatted like buddies, and a new level of communication opened between them.

Last night, I sat on the bedside of my 15-year-old daughter. Her face was crammed into her pillow. She would cry and then sob. Her world was wobbling. "I'm soooo stressed out," she said between mini-convulsions. Her grades had plummeted in a couple of subjects; she was confused about her two boyfriends; she was worried about her weight; I had scolded her about being on the phone all night when she should have been finishing her algebra; and she was exhausted. When I stroked her hair and told her I was proud of her, she sobbed, "How can you be proud of me? I'm not even proud of myself."

She needed reassurance.

No lectures.

No sermons.

Just reassurance.

 Let's Talk: **What "together activities" have been most successful with your teen?**

4. *We move from reprimanding to reassuring.* Adolescence, remember, is a tough time for teens. They're especially concerned about their body-image—the way they're developing physically, the way they look. They're also concerned about their social status, about being accepted into a group of friends. They don't need massive doses of reprimands from their parents; but they do need tons of reassurance.

Especially from their dads.

Studies have demonstrated that the father-teen relationship often erodes during adolescence more than the maternal relationship. Relationships between fathers and their sons are often remembered as warm during the early years, distant and difficult during the teen years, but improved again as the son becomes an adult. Dr. Craig LeCroy of Arizona State University concluded, "When fathers share a greater degree of intimacy with their children, this will have a positive effect on adolescent development and functioning."[10]

5. *We move from preaching to praying.* Christian parents should always pray for their children, and we should always share the wonders of God's Word with them. But during adolescence, they increasingly need someone who will continually pray for them.

Powerful prayers, as I indicated earlier, are based on Scripture. Suppose you had a teenage son named Peter, for example. Here's a prayer personalized for him from Ephesians 3:16-19:

> *Dear Father, I pray that out of Your glorious riches, You will strengthen Peter with power through Your Spirit in his inner being, so that Christ may dwell in his heart through faith. And I pray that he might become rooted and established in love, and may have power to grasp how wide and long and high and deep Your love is, and may he be filled to the measure with all the fullness of God.*

Or suppose you have a daughter named Erica. Here's a prayer you can offer for her based on Psalm 1:

> *Dear Father, I pray that You will keep Erica from choosing wrong companions. May she not walk in the counsel of the wicked, stand in the way of sinners, or sit in the seat of mockers. But teach her to delight in Your Word, and to meditate on it day and night. Make her like a tree You plant by streams of water, which yields its fruit in season and whose leaf does not wither. May whatever she does prosper.*

Scripture Search: "Prayer-a-phrase" the following verses as a prayer of supplication for your teenager.

> *The Lord bless you and keep you;*
> *The Lord make his face shine upon you*
>   *and be gracious to you;*
>   *the Lord turn his face toward you*
>   *and give you peace (Numbers 6:24-26).*

_____

_____

_____

> *May the God of hope fill you with all joy and peace as you trust in him, so that you may overflow with hope by the power of the Holy Spirit (Romans 15:13).*

_____

_____

_____

May the God of peace, who through the blood of the eternal covenant brought back from the dead our Lord Jesus Christ, that great Shepherd of the sheep, equip you with everything good for doing his will, and may he work in us what is pleasant to him, through Jesus Christ, to whom be glory for ever and ever. Amen (Hebrews 13:20-21).

_____

_____

_____

Compose prayers like that and gradually move from controller to companion; from talking to listening; from spending time to spending more time; from reprimanding to reassuring; and from preaching to praying. As you do, the Lord will work in their lives, and they'll grow in wisdom and stature, and in favor with God and men.

In the process, you'll skirt some storms. You might even be able to loosen your seat belt and enjoy the trip!

P.S. (Practical Suggestions from Chapter 8)

1. Use these questions to evaluate your communication patterns:
   - How much time did I talk with my teenager last week?
   - Did I do more talking or listening?
   - Did I come across as dictatorial and defensive?
   - How frequently do we chat like buddies?
   - How can I improve?

2. Take your teen out for a milk shake and fries. Ask him or her the above questions, and see how their answers compare with yours.

3. Find a hobby or activity to enjoy with your teen. Or locate a mutual hang-out. Find a cafe, for example, that you can claim as your special place with your teen, and frequent it.

4. Let your teen plan the family vacation. Family trips are prime times for parent/teen interaction, but many parents don't plan trips teens enjoy. So give your teenager some guidelines, explain the budget, and let him or her decide about where to go and what to do.

5. Compose a prayer for your teenager. Search the Scriptures for an appropriate passage, and paraphrase into a personalized prayer.

6. Practice saying yes whenever you can. Don't become overly alarmed about minor issues such as trends in clothes or room appearance. Choose your battles carefully so that when you need to say no, they'll respect you for your thoughtful decision rather than an impulsive reaction. Explain, and be loving but firm.

[1]Berger, *The Developing Person Through the Life Span,* 332.

[2]Ibid., 332.

[3]Nanci Hellmich, "1 in 7 Teens Say They've Tried Suicide," *USA Today,* 10 August 1988, D1.

[4]Dan Sperling, "Today's Teens Have It Rough," *USA Today,* 11 September 1988, D1.

[5]Berger, *The Developing Person Through the Life Span,* 332.

[6]"The Age of Ambivalence," *Psychology Today,* May/June 1992, 20.

[7]Karen S. Peterson, "Teens: Parents, You're OK," *USA Today,* 25 August 1990, D1.

[8]Gallup Youth Survey, "Exploding the Myths About Teenagers," *U.S. News and World Report,* 10 February 1986, 80.

[9]Jay Kesler, *Ten Mistakes Parents Make with Teenagers (And How to Avoid Them)* (Brentwood, Tenn.: Wolgemuth & Hyatt, 1988), 2.

[10]Craig Winston LeCroy, "Parent-Adolescent Intimacy: Impact on Adolescent Functioning," Adolescence, Vol XXIII, No. 89, Spring 1988, 140.

Signposts and Speed Bumps

Parents' Ongoing Challenge: Discipline

Parents' Secret Battle: Fatigue

Parents' Secret Weapon: Family Scripture Memory

Painful Parenting: When Your Children Break Your Heart

Rewards in Parenting: Leading Kids to the King

❦ 9 ❦
Parents' Ongoing Challenge: Discipline

Discipline has been called the dirty work of parenting—perhaps our toughest responsibility. I know it's my parental Achilles' heel, the area of child raising where my wife and I most frequently disagree. We're not alone. Marriages have selfdestructed over conflicts involving disciplining the children.

Many parents can't provide a lucid definition for the term. The dictionary is less than helpful, for its first definition for *discipline* is *punishment.* So if someone tells us, "I'm going to discipline my son," we assume the kid's about to "get what's coming to him." But read further down the listing of definitions and you'll find one that describes the sort described in this chapter: "Training that corrects, molds, or perfects the mental faculties or moral character."

Discipline, in other words, differs from punishment. It is training in wisdom, virtue, and self-control. When we say someone is a disciplined person, we mean self-controlled. The goal of child discipline is training (yes, sometimes involving punishment) that empowers our children to be more self-controlled.

How important is self-control? Proverbs 25:28 says:

Like a city whose walls are broken down
is a man who lacks self-control.

A strong, safe, well-guarded city in biblical times had high, thick walls to thwart invaders. Enemies had to camp in the open and send vulnerable troops rushing toward the gates with battering rams where the city's defenders waited to shoot well-aimed arrows and repulse the enemy. The population felt safe, because the walls were unassailable.

But if the walls collapsed like those of Jericho, the enemy could waltz right in, loot the stores, rape the women, kill the men, massacre the children, and burn the town.

Proverbs 25 says that a person's self-discipline is his defense in life. The devil can't touch a self-controlled, well-disciplined life. But if we're undisciplined, indulging our appetites, doing whatever we want, exercising little self-control, then Satan doesn't even have to fire a shot. He can waltz into our lives when he chooses. That's why Peter wrote: "Be self-controlled and alert. Your enemy the devil prowls around like a roaring lion looking for someone to devour. Resist him, standing firm in the faith" (1 Peter 5:8).

 Let's Talk: Does our society value self-control? Why does modern culture seem so unrestrained and self-centered?

Scripture Search: **The apostle Paul expressed concern about the undisciplined culture of Crete. Even the Christians lacked self-control. Study the verses below, and answer the questions.**

An elder [church leader] must be blameless ... hospitable, one who loves what is good, who is self-controlled, upright, holy, and disciplined (Titus 1:6,8).

Why is self-control and discipline important for leaders?

_____

_____

Teach the older men to be temperate, worthy of respect, self-controlled, and sound in faith, in love and in endurance. Likewise teach the older women. ... Then they can train the younger women to love their husbands and children, to be self-controlled and pure. ... Similarly, encourage the young men to be self-controlled (Titus 2:2-6).

Which groups of people are instructed to be self-controlled? Underline them.

Write one way self-control can be taught to another person.

_____

For the grace of God that brings salvation has appeared to all men. It teaches us to say "No" to ungodliness and worldly passions, and to live self-controlled, upright and godly lives in this present age (Titus 2:11-12).

The earlier verses imply that self-control can be taught, especially by older people to younger ones. But according to this verse, who or what is the real teacher when it comes to self-control?

_____

How is self-controlled defined in this verse?

_____

List three implications of these verses for parenting.

1. _____

2. _____

3. _____

Where do we learn self-control? Who lays the foundation of these walls of wisdom within us? Our parents! The Bible says,

Discipline your son, for in that there is hope;
do not be a willing party to his death" (Proverbs 19:18).

What son is not disciplined by his father? ... We have all had human fathers who disciplined us and we respected them for it. How much more should we submit to the Father of our spirits and live! Our fathers disciplined us for a little while as they thought best; but God disciplines us for our good, that we may share in his holiness. No discipline seems pleasant at the time, but painful. Later on, however, it produces a harvest of righteousness and peace for those who have been trained by it (Hebrews 12:7-11).

Dr. Ray Guarendi, nationally known speaker and writer, says: "Self-denial is a quality that is developed from the outside in. That is, kids need parents to impose early limits on them, and only with many years will they more completely be able to self-regulate their desires."[1]

Guidelines

If the goal of discipline is to enhance a child's self-control, how should it be administered? First, *never give undisciplined discipline!* All parents have moments when they feel like "wringing the necks" of their children, or screaming harsh and cutting words in their faces. Don't do it. You cannot teach your child self-control if you're out of control! Unrestrained discipline isn't discipline at all. It's child abuse. We may sometimes be angry when we discipline our children, but we must never allow our anger to overwhelm wisdom and good judgment.

Second, *dad and mom need to be united in discipline.* My wife is stricter than I am with our daughters, and we often become frustrated with each other. We may air our disagreements in private and try to reach common ground, but in front of the girls we try hard to be as one. Even if I disagree with the way Katrina handles a situation, I never undermine her.

After all, she's probably right.

Marital disagreements on issues like discipline have actually strengthened our marriage, for they've enabled us both to become more balanced. Katrina has strengthened my resolve in discipline, and I've helped her relax in dealing with problems. When two people agree on everything, they double their chances of being wrong.

Arriving at a working consensus is especially important—and particularly difficult—in divorced and blended families. Chapters 3 and 4 addressed this, but allow me to remind you of one word. *Communicate.* Put the needs of the children ahead of your feelings, and do your best to find common ground with your ex-spouse and/or your new spouse related to discipline. Remember what Isaiah told King Ahaz: " 'Be careful, keep calm, and don't be afraid. Do not lose heart' " (Isaiah 7:4).

Third, *there is no one-size-fits-all method of disciplining children.* Every child is different, every situation unique. One parent said of his two sons, "With one of them I had to use every technique I could think of, including frequent trips to the woodshed. The other boy had a sensitive and shy spirit, and often just a stern look would do the job."

Finally, *these guidelines work best when combined with wisdom.* James 1:5 says, "If any of you lacks wisdom, he should ask God who gives generously to all without finding fault, and it will be given to him." God is deeply concerned that His children "live self-controlled, upright and godly lives in this present age" and He will give special grace for this purpose upon sincere request. (See Titus 2:12.)

Techniques

How, then, do we discipline our children? Here are seven biblical, effective methods; the first two are foundational to the rest.

1. The Loyalty of Love

First John 3 begins with the words, "How great is the love the Father has lavished on us, that we should be called children of God." John continues: "This is how we know that we love the children of God: by loving God and carrying out his commands. ... And his commands are not burdensome" (John 5:2).

In other words, God lavishes his love on us; and because He loves us, we love Him in return. Our love for Him sparks in us the desire to obey and please Him.

Likewise, the foundational way to create obedient and disciplined children is to love them with such warmth and tenderness that they'll never want to break your heart. Young adults who made it through adolescence without becoming highly rebellious or disobedient have told me, "Well, I was tempted, and I might have given in. But I couldn't stand the thought of what it would do to my parents. I didn't want to break their hearts."

The primary restraint to a child's negative behavior is often his good relationship and communication with parents. When these are present, parents don't need other methods of discipline as frequently.

Remember when Peter denied Christ three times, cursed Him, and abandoned Him? What disciplinary technique did Jesus use to rebuke Peter? Only a glance. Just as the rooster crowed, the Lord turned and looked straight at Peter. And Peter went outside and wept bitterly. Jesus had built such levels of love and loyalty into Peter's heart that the worst punishment Simon could ever experience was to see the pain in the eyes of the One he loved.

 Let's Talk: **From your recollections as a child and as a parent, how effective is this technique?**

Perhaps you're doing your best to develop loyalty in your kids, and they still disobey. What then? Parents need some external disciplines, and the most effective is the reprimand.

2. Reprimand

Words—carefully chosen, lovingly given, plainly spoken—are powerful disciplinary tools. Deuteronomy 4:36 says: "From heaven he made you hear his voice to discipline you."

I read a book recently on getting along with a difficult boss. If all else fails, it said, you may have to resort to a heart-to-heart talk. Find a way, the author suggested, to sit down with your boss and tell him what you need to better perform your job. Calmly express your frustrations, and talk with him openly as one human being to another.

I don't know if that will work with your boss, but it often works with our kids. Sometimes we need to reprimand them on the spot, sometimes even with a shout ("Get out of the street!"); other times we need to sit down with them after the issue has cooled and have a quiet talk.

Sometimes when I've observed unacceptable behavior by one of my girls, I've taken her out for a milk shake and casually broached the subject. The word *casually* is important, because if I trigger her defenses, I've lost my opportunity. So I'm as nonchalant as possible in steering us into the subject. I aim for an easy-going conversation, ending with my child better understanding my concerns. Sometimes, I've managed to discipline her without her even realizing it.

In all honesty, I must admit that my wife calls this the "beating-around-the-bush method." She tends to be more direct, and I'll admit that some occasions (well, many occasions) call for directness.

 Scripture Search: **The writer of Proverbs uses words to discipline his son in advance. What are some of the subjects he addresses? Read the selected verses on the next page and write one of these words or phrases in each blank:**

Words	Hard work	Financial discipline
Faith in God	Anger	Alcohol and Drugs
Peer pressure		

Parents' Ongoing Challenge: Discipline

1. _____ Proverbs 1:10
   My son, if sinners entice you,
       do not give in to them.

2. _____ Proverbs 3:5
   Trust in the Lord with all your heart
       and lean not on your own understanding.

3. _____ Proverbs 10:4
   Lazy hands make a man poor,
       but diligent hands bring wealth.

4. _____ Proverbs 13:11
   Dishonest money dwindles away,
       but he who gathers money little by
          little makes it grow.

5. _____ Proverbs 15:28
   The heart of the righteous weighs its answers,
       but the mouth of the wicked gushes evil.

6. _____ Proverbs 19:19
   A hot-tempered man must pay the penalty;
       if you rescue him, you will have to do
          it again.

7. _____ Proverbs 20:1
   Wine is a mocker and beer is a brawler;
       whoever is led astray by them is not wise.

√ Check the two areas that seem most important to you now in your parent/child interactions.

(Answers: 1. Peer pressure; 2. Faith in God; 3. Hard work; 4. Financial discipline; 5. Words; 6. Anger; 7. Alcohol and drugs)

3. Time-Out

Sometimes talk is insufficient, and in those cases I'll suggest a third method of discipline. When our children disobey, we should sometimes do to them what God did to his disobedient prophet Jonah.

No, I'm not talking about throwing them in the ocean!

The last verse of Jonah 1 says: "The Lord provided a great fish to swallow Jonah, and Jonah was inside the fish three days and three nights" (Jonah 1:17).

He sloshed around in the hot, humid, pitch-black, foul-smelling belly of whatever it was that swallowed him. There was nothing to stand on;

nothing to sit on. His bare feet slid over raw slime, and he floated in a mixture of rotten fish, partially decayed seaweed, and stomach juices. You might say Jonah was floundering in the whale.

What did he do during those three days and nights? Nothing. It was dark, hot, wet, and boring. There was nothing to do but think and pray. He had 72 hours of what modern experts call "time-out."

James W. Varni and Donna C. Corwin have written *Time-out for Toddlers* in which they argue that time-outs, used correctly, should be the main way to discipline kids ages 2 to 10. They suggest that parents "buy a kitchen timer and designate a corner or a boring hallway for the time-out chair. When your child misbehaves, tell him exactly what he's done wrong and tell him to go to the time-out chair. If he doesn't go, grasp his wrist and lead him there. Set the timer for one minute for each year (five minutes for a five-year-old), and make your child sit quietly until the timer has measured off the time. If he gets off the chair before the timer goes off, give him a swat on the rear end, put him back in the chair, and reset the timer without saying a word."[2]

The Lord used this method with Moses' sister on one occasion when she developed a bad attitude. She was placed outside the camp for seven days in a sort of time-out zone before the children of Israel could resume their journey toward the promised land (see Numbers 12).

 Let's Talk: **Have you used this technique with your children? What are its advantages? its limitations?**

4. Consequences and Reparations

Another method of discipline God uses with His disobedient children involves *consequences and reparations*. Do you remember when Samson disobeyed God and foolishly revealed the secret of his superhuman strength? God never directly punished Samson; he just allowed him to feel the consequences of his disobedience.

If you tell your children to gather their toys from the backyard, and they don't, let them learn what happens when the rain drenches their toys, or the dog chews them up.

If they're rude to an adult, let them learn what its like to apologize.

If they break a vase, give them extra jobs to earn money to replace it.

My friend, Rick Polston, told me that his father allowed him to learn an important lesson as a 17-year-old high-school student. One night his dad came into the den and told him it was bedtime.

Rick protested. "Why do I have to go to bed at 9:00? I'm a junior in high school!"

" 'Cause I said so," growled his dad. But later that evening, Mr. Polston came to Rick's bedroom and said he had reconsidered. "You're old enough to determine your own bedtime," he said, "but just remember that 5:00 a.m. comes early."

The next night, Rick stayed up and watched the late news with his parents. After they went to bed, he watched a movie, and then another movie. He finally crashed into bed at 2:30 a.m.

Sure enough, 5:00 a.m. came early. Rick stumbled through the day in a painful, sluggish fog, falling into bed before the supper dishes had been washed. "To this day," Rick told me, "I know that if I'm to function properly at any of my endeavors, I need my rest. Dad let me learn a lesson on my own, and I didn't need lesson number two."

5. Withdrawal of Privileges

This fifth technique works with any age—withdrawing privileges. Teenagers call this "grounding." But it isn't just for teenagers! If your elementary-age child brings home lower grades, he may need less television and more study. If she rides her bicycle beyond her boundaries, lock the bike up for a few days. If he doesn't eat his hamburger, he doesn't get his cookie. If she violates her curfew, she loses car privileges for a week. If he doesn't clean his room, he forfeits his allowance.

Jill Johnson was an energetic five-year-old who wouldn't keep her shoes on. Since the Johnson's house was in a new development, her mother worried about Jill cutting her foot on a nail or on a piece of discarded construction material. After persistent and futile appeals, her mother finally said, "Jill, wearing shoes is a privilege; millions of children around the world don't have any shoes to wear. Since you refuse to wear yours, I'm taking them away for 24 hours."

Jill was embarrassed and upset going to Mothers' Day Out, church, and her friend's house with bare feet. But her mother never again had to nag her to wear her shoes while playing outside.

Scripture Search: Read the following Old Testament passages. What privileges did God withdraw from His erring children? Underline your answers in each verse.

And the Lord God said, "The man has now become like one of us, knowing good and evil. He must not be allowed to reach out his hand and take also from the tree of life and eat, and live forever." So the Lord God banished him from the Garden of Eden (Genesis 3:22-23).

"Not one of the men who saw my glory and the miraculous signs I performed in Egypt and in the desert but who disobeyed me and tested me ten times—not one of them will ever see the land I promised on oath to their forefathers. No one who has treated me with contempt will ever see it" (Numbers 14:22-23).

But the Lord said to Moses and Aaron, "Because you did not trust in me enough to honor me as holy in the sight of the Israelites, you will not bring this community into the land I give you" (Numbers 20:12).

List four privileges that could be temporarily withdrawn to help instill self-discipline in your children.

_____   _____

_____   _____

6. Work

Jill's mother tried a different approach with her son, eight-year-old Shawn. She overheard him using a word on the phone she didn't like. After he finished his conversation, she pulled him aside.

"Shawn," she said, "I heard the word you used, and I know that your friends at school might talk like that. But the Bible says we shouldn't let anything nasty come out of our mouths. To remind you not to use that word again, I'm going to give you a job. It has to do with nastiness. Come on, I'll show you how to do it."

She led Shawn to the bathroom, gave him a toilet bowl brush and cleaner, and gave him the responsibility for cleaning all the commodes in the house every day for a week. She told him she would inspect his work, and if it wasn't done well he'd get another week on the job. For an eight-year-old boy, it was equivalent to stocks and pillory.

All children should have certain tasks to do around the home. Studies show that children who grew up with appropriate chores become happier, more responsible adults. Chores, as such, should be a part of family life—not an occasional punishment. But an extra and perhaps unpleasant chore might sometimes be included among the mix of disciplinary techniques you use with your children and teens. As with Shawn, it can reinforce a needed message.

 Let's Talk: **Have you tried this technique with your children? How effective is it?**

7. Spanking

Spanking is controversial today because of the outbreak of child abuse in our society. I understand the concerns that some experts express, but the Bible suggests that while we must never abuse our children, spanking, properly administered, is an acceptable form of discipline. Proverbs 13:24, for example, says,

> *He who spares the rod hates his son,*
> *but he who loves him is careful to discipline him.*

Admittedly, I've failed in this area. When my daughters were younger, I would occasionally give them a pat on the behind; but only once did I really bend one of them over my knee—and I've worried about it ever since! But Katrina has been much better at it.

We should resort to spanking only in cases of outright defiance or rebellion, only when children are younger (pre-puberty), and only in moderation. Rebellion, the Bible says, is a deep and dangerous flaw in our human nature. If it's allowed to flourish in kids, they may be resentful and rebellious all their lives, resisting all authority including God's. Occasionally, the spirit of rebellion is tamed only by the loving but firm application of appropriate corporal punishment. Proverbs 23:13-14 says, "Don't hesitate to discipline a child. A good spanking won't kill him. As a matter of fact, it may save his life" (GNB).

How does one spank a child? If other forms of discipline fail and the child shows clear signs of defiance, tell him in private, "I'm unhappy with your actions and attitudes. If you don't change immediately, I am going to spank you." Your voice should be firm, but not out of control. If the child doesn't show immediate signs of self-correction, follow through with your promise. If the child is screaming or hysterical, wait out his tantrum. When he's finished, stand him against a wall or turn him over your knee and give his bottom a whack or two, just enough to sting. You need some indication—tears or even the quiver of a chin— that he got the message.

After the spanking, your child will need reassurance that your discipline doesn't cancel your love, so be willing and waiting to administer lots of follow-up hugs and kisses.

 Let's Talk: **What do you think of the description of spanking as discipline? Were you spanked as a child? What impact did it make on you?**

There are many other discipline techniques, but these, I think, are the primary ones: loyalty, reprimands, time-outs, consequences and reparations, withdrawal of privileges, work, and spanking. Most of us make two mistakes in discipline. Either we're too permissive, seldom providing the discipline children need, or we're too harsh, and our children grow resentful and rebellious. God alone gives us the wisdom to be balanced in disciplining our children.

For the grace of God that brings salvation has appeared to all men. It teaches us to say "No" to ungodliness and worldly passions, and to live self-controlled, upright and godly lives in this present age, while we wait for the blessed hope—the glorious appearing of our great God and Savior, Jesus Christ, who gave himself for us to redeem us from all wickedness and to purify for himself a people that are his very own, eager to do what is good (Titus 2:11-14).

P.S. (Practical Suggestions from Chapter 9)

1. Renew your resolve to spend time with your children—going on dates, camping, playing games, being friends. Seek to establish long-term warmth and love in your parent-child relationships so that your children will more easily choose to please and obey you.

2. Tell your kids about the kind of discipline you received as a child. Be honest. If you were abused or harshly treated, tell them. If you received little or no discipline, tell them how that harmed you.

3. If you're married, find a time to discuss this issue with your spouse. Agree together in advance to be calm and objective, seeking to build a rational, consistent, working understanding about the discipline of your child or children. Discuss the different ways each child responds to different techniques of discipline.

4. Discuss the disciplinary techniques described in this chapter with other parents. Swap ideas and find out what works best for them.

5. Devote your personal Bible study to reading through the Book of Proverbs, listing everything it says about the discipline of children.

6. Compose a prayer, asking God for wisdom.

7. If you feel you've disciplined your children in an unwise way, go to them honestly and tell them so. Seek to draw out their feelings, and resolve any past hurts. Apologize to them and tell them of your desire to provide firm, wise discipline in the future.

---

[1]Ray Guarendi, *Back to the Family* (New York: Fireside Books published by Simon & Schuster, 1990), 192.
[2]Nancy Hellmich, "There's No Perfect Way to Raise Perfect Children," *USA Today*, 5 September 1991, 6D.

10
Parents' Secret Battle: Fatigue

Alice grew weary of sitting by her sister on the riverbank. The sun was hot—the books, boring. She was thinking of making a daisy chain when a blur ran past her—a white rabbit with pink eyes and a very proper waistcoat. He drew a pocket watch from his coat and looking at it, muttered to himself,

I'm late! I'm late!
For a very important date!
No time to say, "Hello! Goodbye!"
I'm late! I'm late! I'm late![1]

With that, he jumped down a rabbit hole, and Alice followed right behind, into his inside-out, upside-down world.

Americans have been jumping down the same hole. We're the most hurried, worried society in history, with no time to say "Hello! Goodbye!" even to those we most love. Perhaps today's greatest threat to the family isn't humanism, secularism, satanism, or atheism. Perhaps it's a white rabbit with a pocket watch.

"The Annals of Internal Medicine recently reported that 24 percent of people surveyed complained of fatigue that lasts longer than two weeks. Fatigue is now among the top five reasons people call the doctor. People are frayed by the inescapable pressure of technology," observes *Newsweek,* "frazzled by the lack of time for themselves, their families, their PTAs, and church groups."[2]

Another study found that 30 to 50 percent of Americans suffer from sleep deprivation. A hundred years ago, people slept an average eight to nine-and-a-half hours per night. Today? Less than seven hours.[3]

The problem isn't limited to adults, for teenagers tend to follow their parents into the fog of fatigue. Teens need 9 to 11 hours of sleep (as much or more than elementary children), but they get far less. The result? More conflicts with parents, greater emotional volatility, falling asleep in class, lower grades.

American society runs nonstop, 24 hours a day. Nearly one in five employees work nonstandard hours, and more than a thousand different work schedules are being used in industrial and commercial enterprises. Stores, banks, offices are open day and night. Increasing numbers of child-care centers operate 24 hours a day for those homes in which parents can't "tag team" their parental duties.

All this profoundly impacts child rearing. The amount of meaningful time parents spend with their children is shrinking. Furthermore, tired people have fewer emotional reserves. They snap more easily, exhibit more grouchiness, and overreact more quickly. That isn't good for marriage, it isn't good for parenting, and it isn't good for children.

Let's Talk: **How big a problem is fatique for you and your family? Has modern technology (beepers, cable television, microwave ovens, fax machines, computers, cellular phones) helped or hindered you in creating quality together time for your family?**

Recently, I rose before the sun, pulled on my gym clothes, raced to the health club and pumped the bicycle while watching the news and reading the paper. I zoomed by the fast-food restaurant so they could throw a low-fat muffin to me through the window. I zipped and zagged through rush-hour traffic, poured over papers and problems all morning, then crammed a high-fat sandwich into my mouth between phone calls. Ditto for the afternoon. I dragged home that evening exhausted, returned phone calls, cooked supper, washed dishes, helped the girls plod through impossible stacks of homework, finished the paperwork in my briefcase, and dropped into bed about midnight.

As I fell asleep, I wondered, *Is this really what Jesus had in mind when he talked about the abundant life?* (See John 10:10.)

How, then, does the Lord address this problem?

Hidden in the letter to the Ephesians are some often neglected spiritual secrets of highly effective parenting:

Be very careful, then, how you live—not as unwise but as wise, making the most of every opportunity, because the days are evil. Therefore do not be foolish, but understand what the Lord's will is (Ephesians 5:15-17).

Based on these concepts, here are four passwords for getting out of the rabbit's world.

Scan

Ephesians 5:15 says, "Be very careful, then, how you live—not as unwise but as wise." We must step back and scan our lives in the light of God's Word, distinguishing the non-pressing essentials from the nonessential pressing. Many couples work day and night to sustain a lifestyle they haven't time to enjoy. Many families sacrifice irreplaceable, quality time with God and family on the altar of materialism.

We're reading Matthew 6:19-21 backwards. Jesus warned in that chapter, "Do not store up for yourselves treasures on earth, where moth and rust destroy, and where thieves break in and steal. But store up for yourselves treasures in heaven, where moth and rust do not destroy, and where thieves do not break in and steal. For where your treasure is, there your heart will be also."

He didn't mean that we shouldn't work hard to provide for our families' needs, for Deuteronomy 8:18 reminds us the Lord gives us "the ability to produce wealth." The Books of Proverbs and 2 Thessalonians warn us against laziness. Jesus *was,* however, cautioning against overevaluating the toys and treasures of earth. He continued:

Do not worry about your life, what you will eat or drink; or about your body, what you will wear. Is not life more important than food, and the body more important than clothes? Look at the birds of the air; they do not sow or reap or store away in barns and yet your heavenly Father feeds them. … See how the lilies of the field grow. They do not labor or spin. Yet I tell you that not even Solomon in all his splendor was dressed like one of these (Matthew 6:25-26, 28-29).

The Lord then indicated that frantic, overtaxing efforts to accumulate material possessions betray our lack of confidence in His ability to provide. Perhaps Jesus was remembering the Old Testament's rendering of the same point:

It is useless to work so hard for a living,
*   getting up early and going to bed late.*
For the Lord provides for those he loves, while they are asleep
*   (Psalm 127:2, GNB).*

Then Christ punched his point home: " 'But seek first his kingdom and his righteousness, and all these things will be given to you as well' " (Matthew 6:33).

Many of us reverse the process: "My spouse and I work multiple jobs to pay the bills and meet our obligations; we're facing a lot of demands in life, and time is tight. But if we have any left over—if we can find a free Sunday here or there—we'll seek the kingdom of God and His righteousness."

That attitude's nothing but a shovel for digging deeper into the rabbit hole. We'll never get out until we scan our lives and see what God sees—an urgent need for proper priorities. We've got to realize that if we don't accomplish anything else in life—if we never have a new automobile or a house on the lake—at least we're going to invest time with the Lord each day and each week; and we'll find quality time with those we love the most.

Scripture Search: The Bible uses the word *rest* frequently to describe the trusting and calm spirit that Christians should possess. Read the following selected verses and underline *rest* each time it is used.

"Six days you shall labor, but on the seventh day you shall rest; even during the plowing season and the harvest you must rest" (Exodus 34:21).

My soul finds rest in God alone;
my salvation comes from him (Psalm 62:1).

He who dwells in the shelter of the Most High
will rest in the shadow of the Almighty (Psalm 91:1).

"Come to me, all you who are weary and burdened, and I will give
you rest. Take my yoke upon you and learn from me, for I am gen-
tle and humble in heart, and you will find rest for your souls"
(Matthew 11:28-29).

"Come with me by yourselves to a quiet place and get some rest"
(Mark 6:31).

Based on these truths, what is one thing you can do to cultivate a deep sense of inner, spiritual rest?

_____

_____

The first step to regaining management of your life is to step back, take some time, and in prayer ask God to help you evaluate your current lifestyle. Executives learn to keep time-logs, jotting down their activities every 15 minutes for a week. Some couples take a day off, spending time talking through their commitments and involvements, evaluating their priorities and pressures. I take a couple of days off each fall, going to a cabin in the woods to pray and think through my life's agenda for the coming year. However you do it, stop in your tracks long enough to put yourself under God's time-scanning machine.

Of course, when we start evaluating and rearranging our priorities, we'll have to do some pruning. That leads to the second password for getting out of the rabbit hole: *Ban*.

Ban

Most of us are doing a lot of things that wiser priorities would ban. If we're going to take time for a daily devotional walk with the Lord, for worship and involvement in his church, and for our families, we've got to slice other items from our schedule. Every computer and word processor has a delete button, and wise writers push it often. William Zinsser says, "Clutter is the disease of American writing. We are a society strangling in unnecessary words, circular constructions, pompous frills and meaningless jargon. ... The secret of good writing is to strip every sentence to its cleanest components."[4]

The same is true for life. That's why Paul told the Ephesians, "Be very careful, then, how you live—not as unwise but as wise, making the most of every opportunity, because the days are evil. Therefore, do not be foolish, but understand what the Lord's will is" (Ephesians 5:15-17). Strip life to its cleanest components, to its top priorities.

In light of that, ask yourself:

- Must our children be in all those extra-curricular events?
- Do we really need these purchases we're making?
- How can we simplify our lifestyle to reduce expenses?
- Must we have all these credit cards?
- Can our car last another year before replacement?
- Which is more important—cleaning the closet or rocking the baby?
- Are cable television, call-waiting, and car phones eroding my personal and family time by increasing my exposure to interruptions?
- If I'm so busy that I don't have time for church—and if I'm so strapped that I don't have money to give God—are my resources under the Spirit's control?

 Let's Talk: **What are the duties, jobs, ministries, tasks, relationships, organizations, causes, and obligations in which Jesus Christ could have become involved during His three years of active service on earth? How do you explain His priorities in light of His choices?**

Can

After scanning and banning, ask yourself what commitments you can wisely make. What high-priority items can we return to our schedules if we delete unnecessary ones? What is the will of God for our lives?

We know several things from Scripture about God's will: God wants us to worship Him daily at home and weekly at church and to be engaged in a meaningful personal ministry. God wants us to invest time with our spouses and children. God wants us to meet legitimate, necessary financial needs of our families. And God wants us to enjoy some personal time in recreation and rest.

We know a fifth thing, too—God has given each of us just enough time to accomplish His perfect will. That introduces the final password for escaping the rabbit hole: *Plan.*

 Let's Talk: **If you had 10 extra hours a week, how could you most wisely invest them?**

Plan

"See then that ye walk circumspectly, not as fools, but as wise, redeeming the time" (Ephesians 5:15-16, KJV). That doesn't happen automatically; it requires planning, and when you combine planning and time, you're putting together a schedule, a calendar.

Scripture Search: **Read the following Scripture. Suppose you are leading a time management seminar. Write two keys from these passages you could use as a basis for your remarks.**
"See then that ye walk circumspectly, not as fools, but as wise, redeeming the time" (Ephesians 5:15-16 KJV).

The length of our days is seventy years—
or eighty, if we have the strength;
yet their span is but trouble and sorrow,
for they quickly pass, and we fly away (Psalm 90:10).

Teach us to number our days aright,
that we may gain a heart of wisdom (Psalm 90:12).

Key 1 _____

Key 2 _____

My ***first key*** to redeeming my time is a calendar. "The appointment calendar," claims Eugene Peterson, "is the tool with which to get unbusy."[5] A well-tended calendar lets us lock priority items into the flow of our lives; it gives us ammunition to say no to lesser things.

Suppose, for example, I need to spend time with one of my daughters, and we decided to attend a dog show. Imagine someone calling me that morning and saying, "We're in a pinch. Our speaker for tonight's meeting canceled, and we need you to address our executive group on the subject of quality family time."

If I said, "I can't speak to your executives about quality family time because I'm going to the dogs tonight," they'd be offended. But I can say, "I'm sorry; my calendar won't allow it." There's no question about that. In our day, everyone respects the appointment schedule. It's the law of the land, and we can use that to our advantage.

The secret to using a calendar is to plan your week the week before, and plan your day the night before. Every Friday, I meet myself for lunch, nibble a sandwich, review my goals and priorities, survey the coming week's events; and lock the essentials into my schedule.

Similarly, every night I review my schedule for the coming day and plan my time wisely. Sure, interruptions happen. But after I've done my best to minimize them, I accept the rest as from the Lord.

The ***second key*** to redeeming time? Guard your family time. When scheduling for the approaching week, block out lunch with your spouse and a night with your kids. Establish some weekly family traditions.

Each Friday, for example, is our "family night." We often go out to eat, rent a video, or attend an event of some sort. If we can't be together on Friday, we switch to another night.

I also try to guard the bedtime hours. I once heard a minister brag of being so "dedicated to God's work" that he scheduled meetings and visits until late every evening. He crowed that he had never gotten home before his children were in bed.

No wonder his kids have suffered problems.

All hard-working sales representatives, homemakers, executives, coaches, and ministers have to occasionally schedule evening meetings and calls. Many parents work odd shifts, and all of us struggle to preserve time with our children. But nothing—short of daily time with God—is more important than family time, no matter what we have to delete from our never-ending "to do" lists. One study of successful and unsuccessful executives indicated that "a characteristic of failing executives is their readiness to sacrifice their family lives to their occupational lives." Successful executives, on the other hand, found ways to preserve time for themselves and for their families.[6]

When Bill Clinton became president, his chief of staff said making sure the president had time each day to exercise was his first goal. The second was getting the him home each night for dinner with his family. The third was keeping him on schedule. "Those are things," said Thomas McLarty, "that are important to the success of the presidency."

Leadership Journal interviewed George McKinney, a pastor and church planter in California, about his ministry, asking him, "How have the time pressures of ministry impacted your family?" He told of the early years of his ministry when, in addition to planting a church, he held jobs as a probation officer, social worker, and psychotherapist. He had to supplement his income by catching a bus to another area and washing dishes at a restaurant for $1.25 an hour. For 10 years, he worked 16- to 18-hour days.

But he had a plan for spending time with his family. He rose at six each morning, prepared a family breakfast, and spent an hour and a half with his kids before the beginning of the day, before he was worn out. Then he took them to school.

"Three of my sons are now preparing for the ministry," he said. "One teaches in our school, and another is a senior in college. Our great relationships are due to those first ten years when we spent our early mornings praying, laughing, singing, telling stories, eating together."[7]

We find time for what's important to us. Where our treasure is—including our time—there will our hearts be also (see Matthew 6:21).

Make regular time for your family. Block it out and lock it in.

The ***third key*** to redeeming time is to share household chores, and to do it with a good attitude. If both partners work outside the home, then both are equally responsible for the domestic duties inside the home. My wife has recently taken a part-time job at a nearby store, so I'm doing more of the cooking, grocery shopping, and housekeeping—tasks I'm learning to (more-or-less) enjoy. The surest way to foster resentment in marriage, especially in two-paycheck homes, is for one partner (guess which one!) not to carry his share of the household load.

The *fourth key?* Learn the 14th and 15th letters of the alphabet: N-O!

A *fifth key* is to make the most of odd moments. None of us would think of tossing our loose pocket change in the trash every evening, but many of us throw away miscellaneous moments when we're waiting for someone or stuck somewhere. Begin the habit of carrying around some Bible verses to memorize, or a small magazine to read, or a little project to work on.

Sixth, redeem time by creating buffer zones around you. You can't expect to escape the rabbit's world if you continually overbook your calendar. Preserve some time for yourself and some time for rest. Jesus once told the disciples, " 'Come with me by yourselves to a quiet place and get some rest' " (Mark 6:31). For there were many coming and going, and they did not even have time to eat.

The current term for this is *cocooning.* In the Bible, it's a *Sabbath.* In sports, it's called *time-out.* In music, it's an *interlude;* in the theater, *intermission;* and at bars, *happy hour.* Academia calls it a *sabbatical,* and the military has various terms for it: *R&R, shore-leave, liberty, furlough.* Travelers call it *rest stops.* Auto racers call it *pit stops,* and auto mechanics call it *recharging the battery.* Writers think of it as *Walden Pond.* In the media, it's called *We'll be back in a moment.*

Whatever you call it, you've got to have it. Jesus frequently withdrew from the multitudes for the quietness, the solitude, and to recharge His batteries. If He needed it, we badly need it.

Buffer zones are necessary transitions between work and home. When you drag yourself in from a frazzled day at work, you're in no condition to immediately make a positive impact on your family. You need a few quiet minutes to make an emotional transition, for Isaiah reminds us, " 'In quietness and in confidence shall be your strength' " (Isaiah 30:15, KJV).

Before getting home, try spinning a cocoon in your car. Most people curse rush-hour traffic, but Deuteronomy 23:5 claims the Lord can turn curses into blessings. Roll up the windows, leave the smog and noise outside, turn on gentle Christian music, and meditate on a tranquil passage of Scripture such as Psalm 23. Carpooling is good for the environment but not for the soul. After exposure to stressful coworkers, demands, and deadlines all day, we need quiet time alone with ourselves and our Savior. We need replenishing. Turn off the nerve-shattering headlines and pulsating music. Transform your car's interior into green pastures and still waters. Let the Shepherd restore your soul.

However you do it, create some buffer zones.

That leads to the *seventh key* to redeeming time: Guard your time with the Lord. Someone said, "If the devil can't make you bad, he'll make you busy." When we become too busy for the Master, we develop a soul-withering complex, busy-ness birthing barrenness.

For many years, I've devoted the first half-hour or so in the morning to my quiet time. I jot a few notes in my journal, read a passage in my

Bible, find a fresh verse for the day, and share my needs with the Lord in prayer. My wife does the same, for we realized long ago that our relationship would never grow deeper than our walk with our Father.

Prayer "is the key to the morning and the bolt to the evening."

"A day hemmed in prayer," one woman said, "will never come unravelled." Bible reading and prayer are essential to *scanning* your life and evaluating your priorities. Then, you *ban, can,* and *plan.* You can take control of your life, and manage your time in the light of God's will.

Jesus lived a shorter time than most of us and finished a far larger task. We can all do the same. So, "Be very careful, then, how you live—not as unwise but as wise, making the most of every opportunity, because the days are evil. Therefore, do not be foolish, but understand what the Lord's will is" (Ephesians 5:15-17).

 Let's Talk: **What other time-saving tips have worked for you? What creative ways has your family found to spend time together?**

 ## P.S. (Practical Suggestions from Chapter 10)

1. Schedule a date with your spouse at a restaurant that serves a relaxed four-course meal. Talk about your family's schedule and the time demands on each member. Use these questions:
   • Are we wise stewards of the time God gives us?
   • What would most improve the pace of our particular lifestyle?
   • Is there anything non-essential we can cut from our schedule?
   • Do we invest adequate time with each another?

2. Plan a family vacation. Block off as much time as you reasonably can. Beware of a trip that will exhaust you physically or financially; choose a place and a pace that brings your family togetherness and fun. Arrive home two days before you have to return to work.

3. Buy a personal calendar. Begin the habit of planning each day and each week in advance.

4. Study a book or listen to a tape on time management.

5. Purchase calming Christian music for your car's entertainment system. Instrumental selections allow you to pray or meditate on Scripture while listening to them.

[1]*Walt Disney's Alice in Wonderland,* 1951. Based on the book by Lewis Carroll. Video.
[2]LynNell Hancock, "Breaking Point," *Newsweek,* 6 March 1995, 58.
[3]Nanci Hellmich, "Wake-up Call for the Sleep Deprived," *USA Today,* 25 May 1995, D1.
[4]William Zinsser, *On Writing Well* (New York: Harper & Row, 1985), 7.
[5]Eugene H. Peterson, *The Contemplative Pastor* (Dallas: Word Books, 1989), 31.
[6]R. Alec Mackenzie, *The Time Trap* (New York: McGraw-Hill Book Co., 1972), 10.
[7]Brian Larson and Mark Galli, "Time and Money: Spending the Family Fortune," *Leadership Journal,* Fall 1992, 134-136.

∽ 11 ∽
Parents' Secret Weapon: Family Scripture Memory

The most important thing your child possesses is the rotten cauliflower sitting between his ears! That, at least, is what the human brain resembles, a three-pound blob of gray pulp that has been called the most incredible creation in God's universe. It's a fabulous, living supercomputer with unfathomable circuitry and unimaginable complexity. It is a collection of billions of neurons, each as complex as a small computer—imagine having 100 billion computers inside your skull—and each of these neurons consists of a central nerve-cell core attached to a long tail and several thousand wispy dendrites. The dendrites reach out to make contact with other dendrites, and the number of connection points between them is perhaps one quadrillion in every human brain. The number of connections within a single brain, scientists tells us, rivals the number of stars and galaxies in all the universe. Your child's mind is valuable beyond belief.

That's why Satan wants it so badly.

Since 1939 when NBC began regular network broadcasts, America's television airwaves have grown more corrupt season by season. One taboo after another has fallen, until nudity, profanity, violence, and humanism are now pumped like raw sewage into our living rooms. A CBS television executive recently claimed that TV simply reflects the country's behavior, not causes it. "America has matured, and we have to accept that," he said.[1]

Have you ever wondered what our entertainment industry means when it claims that particular shows or movies are for "mature audiences only"? They package senseless violence, four-letter words, and immoral sexuality for "mature" audiences. Mature in what way? Morally mature? Spiritually mature? Intellectually mature? What's mature about abandoning yourself to your hormones, stuffing your mouth with four-letter words, and blowing people to smithereens with machine guns? Does that sound mature to you?

Things are no better on the radio, the information superhighway, or in many magazines—even comic books for children.

Making matters worse, much of today's school curricula requires continual monitoring by Christian parents and teachers. We are living in a post-Christian era. We live among men and women with post-modern philosophies.

 Let's Talk: **How much time each day is the television on at your house? How do you feel about your children's favorite shows? What messages are molding their minds? Do you have rules for the TV?**

The mind, then, is the spiritual battleground on which victory or defeat occurs, and whoever, whatever captivates our children's thoughts will be their master. Emerson once said, "A man is what he thinks about all day long." The Roman philosopher Marcus Aurelius noted, "Our life is what our thoughts make it."[2] The Bible says, "As he thinketh in his heart, so is he" (Proverbs 23:7, KJV).

The reason? Thoughts produce acts, acts produce habits, and habits produce character. That's why Isaiah promised, "Thou wilt keep him in perfect peace, whose mind is stayed on thee" (26:3, KJV), and the book of Hebrews tells us to "fix our thoughts on Jesus, the apostle and high priest whom we confess" (Hebrews 3:1). How do we empower our children to "stay their minds" and "fix their thoughts" on the Lord? How, in a world of diseased minds, can our kids keep theirs pure?

Scripture Search: **Read the following verses.**

Matthew 15:19-20
"For out of the heart come evil thoughts, murder, adultery, sexual immorality, theft, false testimony, slander. These are what make a man 'unclean.' "

Romans 1:21-2
Although they knew God, they neither glorified him as God nor gave thanks to him, but their thinking became futile and their foolish hearts were darkened. Although they claimed to be wise, they became fools. ... Therefore God gave them over in the sinful desires of their hearts.

2 Corinthians 4:4
The god of this age has blinded the minds of unbelievers, so that they cannot see the light of the gospel of the glory of Christ, who is in the image of God.

Philippians 3:18-20
For, as I have often told you before and now say again even with tears, many live as enemies of the cross of Christ. Their destiny is destruction, their god is their stomach, and their glory is in their shame. Their mind is on earthly things. But our citizenship is in heaven. And we eagerly await a Savior from there, the Lord Jesus Christ.

Colossians 1:21
Once you were alienated from God and were enemies in your minds because of your evil behavior.

Complete this multiple-choice quiz by √ checking the answer that best completes each sentence.

1. Murder, immorality, and slander ...
❑ a. can be blamed on the media.
❑ b. can all be blamed on Satan.
❑ c. come out of the human heart.
❑ d. happen because we choose the wrong friends.

2. The thinking of this world is ...
❑ a. sophisticated.
❑ b. wise, leading to a golden age of human progress.
❑ c. futile and dark.
❑ d. eager to obey God.

3. The minds of unsaved people have been blinded by ...
❑ a. Satan, the god of this world.
❑ b. radio and television preachers.
❑ c. a false educational system.
❑ d. the Antichrist.

4. Christians are different from the unsaved primarily in ...
❑ a. the way they dress.
❑ b. their schedules on Sunday.
❑ c. their views about current issues.
❑ d. the way they think.

5. Those who do not receive Christ as Savior are God's ...
❑ a. enemies.
❑ b. friends.
❑ c. sheep.
❑ d. projects.

(Answers: 1.,c.; 2.,c.; 3.,a.; 4.,d.; 5.,a.)

We have a secret weapon—Scripture memory. "I have hidden your word in my heart," said the psalmist, "that I might not sin against you" (Psalm 119:11). "Let the word of Christ dwell in your richly," said Paul in Colossians 3:16. "Write them [my teachings] on the tablet of your heart," says the Lord in Proverbs 7:3.

Suppose you dip a sponge into a pitcher of beer and squeeze it. Will pure water gush out? Of course not. If our children's minds are saturated with questionable movies, novels, music, humanistic theories, and worldly entertainment, what is going to flow out? The answer is clear.

Charles Spurgeon said, "To keep chaff out of a bushel, one sure plan is to fill it full of wheat; and to keep out vain thoughts, it is wise and prudent to have the mind stored with choice subjects for meditation."[3]

What Scripture Memory Can Do for Children

What specifically can Scripture memory do for children? First, it can help your child come to Christ. Paul reminded Timothy, "From infancy you have known the holy Scriptures, which are able to make you wise for salvation through faith in Christ" (2 Timothy 3:15).

Verses like John 3:16, Romans 6:23, and Luke 2:11 plant the seed of salvation in children's hearts. Baroness Leja Messenger was residing in her 300-room Latvian castle when the Russian revolution came. One day a 15-year-old soldier, covered with bloody rags, was carried by stretcher into the great ballroom of her home, an explosion having torn into his skull and legs. The baroness, kneeling beside him, asked if he had a last message.

"No," he gasped, "but would you help me pray?"

Her mind scrambled vainly to remember the Lord's Prayer as she looked frantically for a priest. None was near. Suddenly she recalled John 3:16, taught to her by a nun years before. " 'For God so loved the world that he gave his one and only Son, that whoever believes in him shall not perish but have eternal life' " (John 3:16). As those words suddenly flashed to mind, she found herself quoting it to the boy. With his dying breath, he trusted those words. She later said, "He died believing in Christ—and I lived believing."

Second, memorized Scripture not only plants seed but strengthens a child's soul. The Bible provides the thoughts and values of the Almighty, and as we memorize and meditate on its verses, we begin to think God's thoughts, to share His perspective.

Billy Graham tells of a missionary imprisoned by the Japanese in China. The prisoners in the concentration camp were forbidden to read the Scriptures, and those found with a Bible were executed. But she had a copy of the Gospel of John, and in the evening in bed she pulled the covers over her head and, using a flashlight, memorized it a verse at a time. She went to sleep night after night in this way.

After she memorized a page, she tore it out and when she washed her hands she dissolved it in the soap and washed it down the drain. "In this way," she said, "John and I parted company."

She shared her secret with a *Time* reporter just before the prisoners were freed. Later, as the prisoners walked through the gates of the prison camp, the reporters noticed how listless and lifeless they seemed. All of them, that is, except this little missionary who practically glowed. One of the news reporters said, "I wonder if they managed to brainwash her?"

"No," said the *Time* correspondent. "God washed her brain!"[4]

That leads to another benefit of Scripture memory—inner health and happiness. Romans 8:6 says, "The mind controlled by the Spirit is life and peace." Most depression is much simpler and more curable than commonly thought. The real disease may not primarily be childhood conflicts, unconscious anger, or faulty brain chemistry, but negative thinking.

When the Word of God fills our minds, it changes our mind-set, giving us not constant euphoria but a genuine basis for true optimism. The apostle Paul said, "Fill your minds with those things that are good and that deserve praise: things that are true, noble, right, pure, lovely, and honorable. ... And the God who gives us peace will be with you" (Philippians 4:8-9, GNB).

I have a friend who as a child was involved in Scripture memory projects in which she learned about two hundred verses. She said, "I probably couldn't quote each and every Scripture for you word perfect, but I can tell you this—God brings them to mind in my daily walk just when I need encouragement."

Scripture memory also guards our children against temptations. "Thy word have I hid in mine heart," says Psalm 119:11, "that I might not sin against thee" (KJV). Evil is magnetic and mesmerizing, pulling at our children with almost irresistible force, and only the Word of God can empower them to withstand its lure.

Scripture memory builds an arsenal of verses for future ministry, too. Imagine how a quarterback would feel who needed constant time-outs to study the game plan because he hadn't memorized the plays. That's how a Christian feels who can't come up with the right verse in witnessing or counseling. But when our minds are stocked with Scripture, the right words come easily.

I visited a young man once who was near suicide, distressed over his drug and alcohol abuse. Nothing I said seemed to have any effect, and he pleaded, "Just let me die. It's meant to be." Suddenly a verse flashed into my mind, one learned in childhood. "No," I said, "it isn't meant to be." The Bible says, "He is patient with you, not wanting anyone to perish, but everyone to come to repentance" (2 Peter 3:9). For the first time, a faint hope flickered in his eyes, and I credit my friend's eventual recovery, in part, to that moment.

Scripture memory can benefit your kids in other ways, too: giving them increased Bible knowledge, accelerated spiritual growth, and potent truth to counteract the corruption of America's entertainment industry. Verses learned by heart have a cleansing effect, ridding the mind of unclean thoughts and words. As time goes by, Scripture memory can enrich their prayer lives, aid in worship, and give them a stronger sense of God's presence throughout the day. Memorized verses can also help at night, providing powerful antidotes to the fears that sometimes disturb their sleep.

A lady told me of watching a televised documentary during the height of the cold war about the terrifying prospects of nuclear war. She had two small daughters, and after watching the program she couldn't sleep. Fears and dangers flooded her mind. But as she lay in bed, words previously memorized from Psalm 46 came to her forcefully: "God is our refuge and strength, an ever present help in trouble. ... Be still, and know that I am God" (vv. 1, 10). These words had such a calming influence on her that she went to sleep and slept like a baby.

Let's Talk: **Do you still remember any Bible verses memorized in childhood? What are they? How can you help your children memorize Scripture?**

How Children Memorize Scripture

Believe it or not, I learned most of my Bible verses in the public schools of my small mountain town during the 1950s. A kindly gentleman came each week, awarding prizes for verses memorized; the entire class worked on them together. Today, responsibility rests with home and church. Every family will take a different approach, but here is a list of ideas for you and your kids to consider:

• *Choose a verse-of-the-week, post it on the refrigerator and in all bedrooms.* After selecting a verse for the family, briefly explain it to the children. You might say, "This week's verse is 2 Corinthians 9:7. It was written by the apostle Paul to the Christians in Corinth. Let's find this city on the map in the back of your Bible." You might then explain that chapters 8 and 9 are devoted to the importance of giving a portion of our income to God. Then you can discuss the verse itself, "Each man should give what he has decided in his heart to give, not reluctantly or under compulsion, for God loves a cheerful giver."

Next memorize the verse customizing the memorization techniques to your child's aptitudes. But keep it simple. If your child writes the verse out and reads it several times, and reviews it each night, it will begin to settle easily and naturally into his memory bank.

The third phase of memorizing is obedience. Ask your child, "Now, how can we obey this verse?" She'll probably beat you to the punch by suggesting giving a portion of her allowance each week to the Lord.

• *Make Bible trees for your preschoolers' rooms.* You can "plant" a fallen tree branch in a pot of sand or attach a cardboard tree to the wall. As your child learns verses, print them on leaves of construction paper and let him attach them to the tree.

• *Take your children on a shopping excursion for a set of colorful three-by-five inch cards with an appropriate card box.* Or find a plastic picture frame or photo album. Or you might consider a baseball card album with wallet-sized cards. Tell your kids these items are for their newest collection. Then have your children copy Bible verses onto their cards. Find a regular time to work on memorizing these verses, reading them through and breaking them down phrase by phrase, learning each part before continuing to the next. Use spare moments in the kitchen or car to brush up on the verses. As one verse is learned, go on to the next until entire passages are committed to memory. As each verse is learned, file it away in their boxes or albums.

• *Keep a list of the verses memorized so as your child grows and matures he can build on them by memorizing entire passages.* Along the way, don't be afraid to use incentives. Ruth Bell Graham once had a teacher who offered students $5.00 to memorize the Sermon on the Mount. Ruth spent many hours going over Matthew 5, 6, and 7, and when the time came to recite it, she made one mistake and got $4.50.

"But," she now says, "I wouldn't take one thousand times that amount in place of having memorized it."[5]

 Let's Talk: **What obstacles stand between your family and Scripture memory? What hinders you from taking the lead to encourage members of your family to memorize Scripture?**

Use any translation you wish, and use it consistently.

Most of all, make it a priority. Make up your mind to do it. God placed a wonderful "memorizer" in children's minds. They can learn a verse in 10 minutes that may take you and me all week to master. And they'll remember it longer and quote it more perfectly.

A friend of mine, hearing my young daughter quoting 1 Corinthians 13, the love chapter, asked her to recite it at his wedding.

She agreed; I panicked. *What if she forgets it?* I thought. *What if she gets stage fright? What if she draws a blank?* I drilled her day and night, lectured her about deep breathing exercises, wrung my hands in apprehension; and at the wedding I was a nervous wreck.

She didn't miss a word.

Children seldom do. Memorizing Scripture comes as easily to them as chewing gum, and entire passages committed to memory will be retained a lifetime.

Don't wait another day to start.

 ## P. S. (Practical Suggestions from Chapter 11)

Here are some starter verses for your family to memorize. Select simple portions from the verses for younger children.

John 3:16 — "For God so loved the world that he gave his one and only Son, that whoever believes in him shall not perish but have eternal life."

Romans 6:23 — For the wages of sin is death, but the gift of God is eternal life in Christ Jesus our Lord.

Psalm 119:11 —
I have hidden your word in my heart
that I might not sin against you.

Genesis 1:1 — In the beginning God created the heavens and the earth.

John 15:12 — "My command is this: Love each other as I have loved you."

John 15:14 — "You are my friends if you do what I command you."

Colossians 3:20 — Children, obey your parents in everything, for this pleases the Lord.

Psalm 122:1 —
I rejoice with those who said to me,
> *"Let us go to the house of the Lord."*

Psalm 100:1-3 —
Shout for joy to the Lord, all the earth.
> *Worship the Lord with gladness;*
> *come before him with joyful songs.*
Know that the Lord is God.
> *It is he who made us, and we are his;*
> *we are his people, the sheep of his pasture.*

Psalm 23:1-3 —
The Lord is my shepherd, I shall not be in want.
> *He makes me lie down in green pastures,*
he leads me beside quiet waters,
> *he restores my soul.*
He guides me in paths of righteousness for his name's sake.

1 John 4:7 — Dear friends, let us love one another, for love comes from God.

Matthew 6:9-13 —
" 'Our Father in heaven,
hallowed by your name,
your kingdom come,
your will be done on earth as it is in heaven.
Give us today our daily bread.
Forgive us our debts,
> *as we also have forgiven our debtors.*
And lead us not into temptation,
but deliver us from the evil one.' "

---

[1]Alan Bash, "Networks Turn Up Volume on Foul Words," *USA Today*, 28 July 1995, 3D.
[2]Dale Carnegie, *How to Stop Worrying and Start Living* (New York: Simon and Schuster, 1948), 89.
[3]Charles Haddon Spurgeon, *John Ploughman's Talks* (Grand Rapids: Baker Book House, 1976), 53.
[4]Billy Graham, *How to Be Born Again* (Waco: Word Books, 1977), 44-45.
[5]Ruth Bell Graham, *It's My Turn* (Old Tappan, N.J.: Fleming H. Revell Company, 1982), 172.

∾ 12 ∾
Painful Parenting: When Your Children Break Your Heart

I had a prodigal once. Katrina and I took in a young man named Mark who had struggled with alcoholism and severe drug addiction almost since childhood. For several months we watched him grow in the Lord Jesus, and we gradually grew to love him as a son. His smile captured our hearts, and our three daughters started calling him their "older brother."

When he suddenly returned to his hazy world of hard-core addiction, our hearts shattered like crystal thrown to the floor; and ever since, I've felt a deep-reaching sympathy for parents of prodigals.

The Bible is filled with stories of good people who had problems with their children. Adam and Eve suffered heartbreak because of Cain. Noah had problems with Ham. Isaac was grieved because of Esau, and Jacob had one trauma after another because of his disobedient and thoughtless sons. The two sons of Aaron were killed because of their foolishness; and Gideon, one of Israel's greatest judges, had 70 sons who were killed by their devious half-brother. Samuel's sons weren't fit to replace him as leaders of Israel, and all but one of David's kids gave him nothing but trouble.

I could go on and on, because the Bible is full of wayward children. But there's one prodigal we think of more than any other, the young man in Luke 15 whose attitude soured for reasons we aren't given. His father undoubtedly tried to talk to him time and again, but perhaps his words provoked angry responses. Night after night the father trudged to his bedroom with a troubled heart, fearing he was losing his son.

Finally the boy left home, trekked to a pagan country, and spent his money on parties and prostitutes. Months, perhaps years, passed, and finally, his money and vitality spent, the young man came to his senses. He set his steps toward home, returning broke, sick, ragged, wiser.

His dad, seeing a speck on the horizon, recognized his wasted son, ran to him, embraced him, forgave him, loved him. He killed the fattened calf and called together his friends and celebrated.

" '[My son] was dead and is alive again,' " he cried. " 'He was lost and is found' " (Luke 15:32).

What Are Parents of Prodigals to Do?
I spent months in paralyzing agony over my young, troubled friend. Sometimes I was so worried I couldn't function at work or home. What else could I do? My "boy" was out of control—playing a dangerous game with lethal amounts of cocaine and alcohol.

The levels of pain I felt drove me to some counselor friends who advised me about handling an alcoholic and handling myself.

I finally learned some rugged lessons about dealing with prodigals; lessons about love, codependency, letting go, and faith in God. But having learned them the hard way, I suddenly realized they were all here in Jesus' story about the wayward son and his dad. Jesus undoubtedly told this simple story to reveal to us the heart of God, yes and to give parents of prodigals a strategy for hope. Notice the responses made by the heartbroken father.

1. He released his son.

Surely the father had tried many times to talk to his son, to reason with him, perhaps in heated or emotional exchanges. But finally the father realized he couldn't control his son's desires.

We come to a point of realizing we can't assume responsibility for another's choices. God gave each of us a mind, and we can't dictate another's decisions. So the father released his son, perhaps helping him gather his things and watching until he disappeared over the horizon. Then he went back to his room, hid his face in his hands, and sobbed.

I'm surprised—and impressed—that the father didn't run after him, crying, begging, or pleading with him. He didn't throw himself before the young man's path like most of us would. The good father realized that he had to allow his son to make the decision to leave and then live with the consequences of that decision.

We never can do things only God can do. The Lord loves our children even more than we do. He's present everywhere, and His providence is all pervasive. He died for our sons and daughters, and we never make a mistake when we turn our burdens over to Him.

Letting go doesn't mean we stop caring. We don't detach from our love for our child. But we detach from the anxiety that cripples us, that destroys our joy and confidence in life. It isn't God's will for our wayward children to ruin our lives as well as their own. I know a heartbroken mother who was told, "Christ died for your son; it isn't necessary for you to die for him, too. Let the Lord handle it."

As I was writing this chapter, I received a letter from a dear friend, writing about his son. He said, "We have been put to the 'tough love' test. We will have to release him when he leaves us this time. He seems to have chosen certain philosophies of life that are contrary to what we have adopted. We cannot support his lifestyle, and I just ask you to pray for us—and for him."

I recently spoke to a dad about his wayward children. He admitted that he may have contributed to their problems, for he was often too busy for them, keeping a hectic travel schedule.

"My first reaction," he said, "was to ask 'Where did I fail?' But I've decided that a parent with a troubled child shouldn't blame himself too much. A lot of good children have come from bad homes, and sometimes bad children can come from good homes. At some point the child must bear the responsibility for his own decisions."

He continued, "I've confessed to the Lord and to my children my failures, and I'm not going to live with that guilt over my head. I've got to start where I am, pray for my kids, love them, and trust the Lord to build a hedge around them to steer them to Himself."

2. He remained concerned for his son's well-being.

I assume the wise father in Jesus' story also released his son into God's keeping through prayers that were unceasing.

Prayer is our greatest tool in child-raising, for it brings the power of highest heaven to bear upon our children's lives. In my experience with Mark, prayer made all the difference. I'll never forget the sobbing depression that enveloped me when I finally found him in a basement apartment, depleted, hopeless, ready to escape the torments of life. He begged me to leave him, to let him die alone of the drug overdose that he said was only a day or two away.

I tried to reason with him, but my tears and appeals seemed to have no effect, and I went home and fell on my face in prayer. There was nothing more I could do. I had seen counselors; I had consulted authorities; I had notified friends. Nothing was left but to pray for a hopeless situation. I'm convinced that my friend's eventual recovery came through prayer and prayer alone.

Such a powerful force is the prayer power of a heartbroken parent's earnest pleas for his or her prodigal, especially when the words are taken directly from Scripture.

In the parable of the prodigal son, for example, I found this phrase in verse 17: " 'When he came to his senses.' " This became a prayer I offered over and over for Mark—"Lord, bring him to his senses. Lord, bring him to himself."

John 17:15 is a potent prayer. Jesus, praying for His troubled disciples, provides us with a prayer for our troubled children: " 'My prayer is not that you take them out of the world but that you protect them from the evil one.' "

Scripture Search: Read the following verses and answer the questions beneath each one.

"When you pray, go into your room, close the door and pray to your Father, who is unseen. Then your Father, who sees what is done in secret, will reward you" (Matthew 6:6)

Where is your best place to pray?_____.

What promise does God make in this verse?

_____

What are its conditions? _____.

We have not stopped praying for you and asking God to fill you with the knowledge of his will through all spiritual wisdom and understanding. And we pray this in order that you may live a life worthy of the Lord and may please him in every way (Colossians 1:9-10).

How often did Paul pray for the Colossians?_____

Why did he ask God to fill them with a knowledge of His will?

_____

Do not be anxious about anything, but in everything, by prayer and petition, with thanksgiving, present your requests to God. And the peace of God which transcends all understanding, will guard your hearts and your minds in Christ Jesus (Philippians 4:6-7).

When we don't pray, we're prone to be _____.
How are we guarded by God's peace when we pray?

_____ and _____

3. He loved unconditionally.

This man deeply loved his son, and nothing in the world could change that. He loved him with a "no-matter-what" kind of love. In Hasidic lore, there's an old story about a father who complained to Baal Shem Tov that his son had forgotten God. "What, Rabbi, shall I do?" The Baal Shem Tov replied, "Love him more than ever."

The father's love leaps off the page in Luke 15:20: " 'While he was still a long way off, his father saw him and was filled with compassion on him; he ran to his son, threw his arms around him and kissed him.' "

Your children may drift away from your teaching and your standards for awhile, but they can never escape your unceasing prayers and unconditional love. Those two things are like the two ends of a horse-shoe-shaped magnet that will draw them back to God.

4. He spoke honestly.

Notice this especially in his response to the older son, who was, in a different way, also a prodigal. "My son," the father said, "you are always with me, and everything I have is yours. But we had to celebrate and be glad, because this brother of yours was dead and is alive again; he was lost and is found" (Luke 15:32).

I know a young man whose father finally had a brutally frank heart-to-heart talk, said, "Son, I'm very afraid for you. You're either going to shape up and sober up; or you're going to be locked up; or you're going to be covered up—in a coffin. It's your decision."

Those words finally got through to the boy, and he turned around.

5. He withdrew strategically.

Speaking honestly helps us act honestly, sometimes withdrawing logistical support from a prodigal, sometimes saying no, especially when he's trying to maneuver us into supporting his negative behavior. Jesus carefully pointed out that the young man's repentance began only after his resources were exhausted and no one gave him anything.

What if the father had sent the boy money? What if the father had heard of his son's poverty and plight? What if the father had said, "I can't let him starve to death. I can't stand to see him suffer. I'll give him enough money to buy a little food, to purchase a little clothing."

The most painful moment with my prodigal occurred about two months into his relapse, while he was still living under our roof. I went to his room, sat on the bed beside him, looked into his blurred eyes, and evicted him from our house. "I can't let you do this to my family any longer, Mark. My daughters can't concentrate in school because they're so worried about you. They're crying themselves to sleep every night. And it isn't doing you any good, either. We love you too much to give you safe haven while you continue drinking and drugging. It just allows you to go on like this without consequence. You'll have to find another place by next week."

He nodded sadly, then told me he didn't have any funds to rent an apartment. He asked if I could loan him some money. I said no. He jumped up, cursed, and told me I hated him. He told me he'd never ask me for anything else as long as he lived. He told me he never wanted to see me again. And after he moved out, it was weeks before he called, wanting to talk. Forcing him to face the consequences of his behavior without bailing him out made him face up to his problems.

I'm not suggesting, of course, to withdraw genuine compassion and prayer. But the father in Luke 15 never wired any money to his foolish son enabling him to continue his foolishness a little longer. Jesus indicated that only by hitting bottom did the boy's heart begin to look toward heaven and toward home.

6. He waited.

So the father released his son. He remained concerned for his son's wel-being, loved unconditionally, and spoke honestly. He exercised rugged love, allowed his son to hit bottom, and waited through long days and longer nights. And he waited

Scripture Search: Read the verses on the next page and complete the questions that follow.

We wait in hope for the Lord;
    he is our help and our shield.
In him our hearts rejoice, for we trust in his holy name.
                                    (Psalm 33:20-21)

Be still before the Lord and wait patiently for him (Psalm 37:7).

I wait for the Lord, my soul waits,
    and in his word I put my hope.
My soul waits for the Lord
    more than the watchmen wait for the morning (Psalm 130:5-6).

Since ancient times no one has heard,
    no ear has perceived,
no eye has seen any God besides you,
    who acts on behalf of those who wait for him (Isaiah 64:4).

These verses tell us there are situations in life too difficult for us to solve by ourselves. We need to entrust them to God in prayer, and then wait for Him to work. What situation in your life right now most fits into this category?

_____

_____

What attitudes of the heart should accompany our waiting?

_____

_____

Waiting on the Lord doesn't mean mindless or wishful thinking; rather it means hoping in His Word. What does *hoping in His Word* mean to you?

_____

_____

Who besides God can help us with impossible problems?

_____

Sometimes it takes a while. Let me introduce you to another friend of mine. His parents were upright citizens, well-to-do, but not rich. His mother was a devoted Christian, but she labored vainly against the influences of her husband, an intemperate and immoral man.

My friend was brilliant in school, making top grades with little effort. But as he sauntered through adolescence, his education began taking second place to his hormones. Against his mother's wishes, he moved out of her home and began rooming with a buddy. He later wrote that he "burned for all the satisfactions of hell," and, in addition to sex and substance abuse, became a petty thief.

He impregnated his girlfriend, and they started living together for the sake of the baby. Meanwhile, he enrolled in the university, surprised his professors with his intelligence, and started dabbling in Eastern mysticism. Soon he was absorbed with his new faith, and though only 19, became its most outspoken exponent. He often debated Christian speakers, brilliantly making his points.

My friend collected his degrees and began a stellar career as an educator, traveling abroad to teach in a major university in Italy. He threw out his live-in lover, kept their son, and planned to marry another woman. Meanwhile, he took up with yet a third lover.

His life was a wreck.

But his mother prayed endlessly for him, year after year. She followed him to Italy where, to her delight, she found a preacher whose intellectual ability attracted her son's interest. But he continued his immoral lifestyle, unable to control his sexual energy, and his health began to break. He was aging beyond his years and on some days, he hardly had enough strength to lecture.

His soul was hurting too, and he grew progressively more depressed. Finally, one day, he came to the end of himself. "What's the trouble with us?" he screamed to a friend. "For all our education, our hearts are empty." He ran out of the room into a park and collapsed under a fig tree, weeping, praying.

Then at last he opened a Bible, finding these words in Romans 13:14, "Clothe yourselves with the Lord Jesus Christ, and do not think about how to gratify the desires of the sinful nature." He stammered out an earnest prayer, asking Christ to be his Savior, and at that moment, he became a changed man.

For over thirty years, his mother had hoped against all odds that he would be saved. For thirty years, she had prayed for that moment; none of her prayers were wasted. As her pastor once told her, "The child of so many tears could not be lost."

I only know my friend through his writings. He lived a millennia-and-a-half ago. He was St. Augustine, one of the most significant leaders in the history of the church of Jesus Christ, the most important figure in post-apostolic Christianity. His mother, Monica, died shortly after his conversion, feeling that her life's work was finally completed.

No prodigal could be more hopeless than my two friends—or than the young man in Jesus' story. Yet the Lord Almighty specializes in impossible missions; He gives hope to the hopeless. That's why we should never lose hope, never give up, and never stop praying.

Ruth Graham put it this way:

For all
who knew the shelter of The Fold,
its warmth and safety
and The Shepherd's care,
and bolted;
choosing instead to fare
out into the cold,
givethe night;
revolted by guardianship.
by Light:
lured
by the unknown;
eager to be out
and on their own;
freed
to water where they may,
feed where they can,
live as they will:
till they are cured,
let them be cold,
ill;
let them know terror;
feed them with thistle,
weed,
and thorn;
who choose
the company of wolves,
let them taste
the companionship wolves
to helpless strays;
but, oh! Let them live—
wiser, though torn!
And wherever,
however, far away
they roam,
follow
and
watch
and
keep–
Your stupid, wayward,
stubborn sheep
and someday
bring them home![1]

P.S. (Practical Suggestions from Chapter 12)

1. If you don't have a prodigal, adopt one. Find a set of hurting parents and pray for them. Visit your local mission or state prison; remember that every troubled person is someone's prodigal; and begin a personal prayer ministry of compassion toward prodigals and those they have disappointed.

2. If you have a prodigal:
   - Begin a study of prodigals in Scripture.
   - Practice the steps outlined in this chapter.
   - Recruit a prayer partner to assist you in praying.
   - At each meal, pray for your prodigal.

3. If your child is involved in drug or alcohol use, locate a support group, and attend it regularly. A well-run group helps members cope with the pain they're already feeling. Your church may be able to suggest an appropriate group for your needs.

4. Don't give up. There are no impossible cases.

---

[1]Ruth Bell Graham, *Prodigals and Those Who Love Them* (Colorado Springs: Focus on the Family, 1991), 15.

❧ 13 ❧
Rewards in Parenting: Leading Kids to the King

One day on a walking tour of Albany, New York, after visiting the State House and rambling through the city's quaint streets, I stopped for lunch on a park bench. I felt someone staring at me. Turning around, I saw a little fellow watching me with intense interest. He appeared to be 11 or 12, eyes big, face crinkled with curiosity.

"What's your name?" he finally asked. Then, "What you eatin'? Where you from? Tennessee? Where's that? What're you doin' here?"

I told him I had come to Albany to preach at a church.

"What does it mean to preach?" he asked.

"It means to tell others about Jesus," I replied.

His eyes widened, and he cupped his hand over his mouth.

"Jesus," he whispered. "Mister, don't you know? That's a cuss word."

Shocked, I realized that the only times this boy heard the name *Jesus* was as a profanity in his home and in his neighborhood.

Compare that little fellow's history with Timothy's upbringing: "From infancy you have known the holy Scriptures, which are able to make you wise for salvation through faith in Christ Jesus" (2 Timothy 3:15).

Scripture Search: Read the following verses.

• *For what I received I passed on to you as of first importance: that Christ died for our sins according to the Scriptures, that he was buried, that he was raised on the third day according to the Scriptures (1 Corinthians 15:3-4).*
• *Always be prepared to give an answer to everyone who asks you to give the reason for the hope that you have (1 Peter 3:15).*
• *"You will receive power when the Holy Spirit comes on you; and you will be my witnesses" (Acts 1:8).*
• *"Come, follow me," Jesus said, "and I will make you fishers of men" (Matthew 4:19).*

Based on what you read, ✓ check the things that are necessary for leading another person to Christ.

❑ A seminary education ❑ The Holy Spirit
❑ An extroverted personality ❑ An inward hope
❑ The ability to preach ❑ A grasp of the gospel
❑ Years of Christian maturity ❑ A commitment to Christ
❑ A silver tongue ❑ Burden for the unsaved

A long list, but much shorter if you didn't check any in the left column.

Every youngster has the right to hear and know the story of Jesus from earliest childhood, and every child deserves the opportunity to receive Christ as Savior. Jesus warned his followers against hindering little children from coming to Him. Jesus spoke in starkest language when, placing a small child near Him, He said:

"If any of you causes one of these little ones who trusts in me to lose his faith, it would be better for you to have a rock tied to your neck and be thrown into the sea" (Matthew 18:6, TLB).

"Beware that you don't look down upon a single one of these little children. For I tell you that in heaven their angels have constant access to my Father. And I, the Messiah, came to save the lost. If a man has a hundred sheep, and one wanders away and is lost, what will he do? Won't he leave the ninety-nine others and go out into the hills to search for the lost one? And if he finds it, he will rejoice over it more than over the ninety-nine others safe at home! Just so, it is not my Father's will that even one of these little ones should perish (Matthew 18:10-14, TLB).

Notice that it was a lamb that was lost. It was a lamb that drove the Shepherd into the mountains, wild and bare. The wording of this passage suggests that it's possible for children to trust in Christ.

The Lord takes children seriously. The Bible says they can glorify God. " 'Have you never read, "From the lips of children and infants you have ordained praise"?' " (Matthew 21:16).

The Bible says they can understand Scripture: "From infancy you have known the holy Scriptures, which are able to make you wise for salvation through faith in Christ Jesus" (2 Timothy 3:15).

The Bible says they can worship and work in God's house: "The boy Samuel ministered before the Lord under Eli" (1 Samuel 3:1).

The Bible says children can give their resources to the Lord: " 'Here is a boy with five small barley loaves and two small fish' " (John 6:9).

And the Bible says that children can come to Christ and be saved: " 'Let the little children come to me, and do not hinder them, for the kingdom of God belongs to such as these' " (Mark 10:14).

 ***Let's Talk:* What's true for children is true for you, too. Are *you* a Christian? If not, will you make that life-changing decision?**

Theologians have argued for centuries about the age at which children can decide to receive Christ as their Savior. During the Middle

Ages, church leaders worried that children might die before becoming Christians, and that fear led to practicing infant baptism. On the other hand, some New England Puritans expected children to grow up in a state of sin and be convicted and converted at maturity.

Early to mid-childhood provides the best opportunities for parents to lead children to Christ. Once a child knowingly sins, he can believe.

Never rush a child into the kingdom, but be sensitive to his spiritual needs and lay a foundation for belief. "Christians seem to be the only ones who believe they should wait to influence children's minds," wrote author David Shibley. "Child abusers don't wait. Neither do humanist educators, false religions and cults, or Satan."[1]

The Christian church has been built by people saved in childhood. For example, during the latter days of the apostles, a boy was born in Smyrna, in today's Turkey, named Polycarp. He became a disciple of the elderly apostle John, and for eight decades, until about A.D. 160, provided powerful leadership to the early church.

When he was 86 years old, a local persecution erupted in Smyrna, and several of his church members were murdered by government officials. Polycarp was singled out as the leader of the church. The authorities seized the old man and threatened him with death if he didn't deny the faith. His reply has pealed through centuries of church history: "Eighty and six years have I served Him, and He hath done me no wrong. How can I speak evil of my King who saved me?"

The governor said, "Then I'll throw you to the beasts."

Polycarp said, "Bring on your beasts."

The governor snarled, "If you scorn the beasts, I'll have you burned."

Polycarp replied, "You try to frighten me with the fire that burns for an hour, and you forget the fire of hell that never goes out."

At that he was tied to a stake and set aflame. As fire lashed his body and carried his soul to heaven, he prayed, "Lord God, Almighty, I praise Thee, I bless Thee, I glorify Thee through Jesus Christ."[2]

Now, how old was this Christian giant at his conversion?

Nine!

He came to Christ when he was nine years old.[3]

In the mid-1800s, an eight-year-old girl in New York City named Eliza Agnew enjoyed geography. As she poured over the maps in her classroom, she spotted an island in the Indian ocean off the southern coast of India—Ceylon, modern Sri Lanka. Ceylon was famous for its pearl fisheries. People the world over traveled there to harvest pearls.

Eliza decided to go there and gather pearls also, but her pearls were children. Eventually the way opened, and she sailed to Ceylon, never to return to America. For 41 years until her death at age 76, she ran a girls' boarding school, teaching over a thousand girls. She is known in missionary history as "The Mother of a Thousand Daughters."

Out of those thousand girls, Eliza personally led six hundred to Christ. Many of them became teachers in village schools; many became wives of pastors, teachers, doctors, and lawyers; many became mothers who brought up their children to know the Lord. Eliza invested her life gathering pearls for the Savior, and she was only eight when the Lord drew her heart to this task.[4]

Each of my three daughters asked Christ into their hearts when they were five. I was also converted about the same age.

My friend Mike Hollifield came to Christ at age 10. At one Sunday evening service, his pastor invited those wishing to become Christians to join him at the front of the church. Several children responded. Mike saw them and went to the front, too, not really thinking about being saved, but just wanting to join his friends. But his parents followed him down and explained in simple terms the meaning of the life and death of Jesus. Mike, finding himself suddenly overwhelmed with emotion, began crying. That evening he gave his heart to the Lord. He later dedicated his life to full-time youth ministry.

We conducted a survey recently at our church among our regular attenders who identify themselves as born-again Christians. We asked them at what age they had trusted Christ as Savior.

- 10 percent were saved at 5 years of age or younger.
- 50 percent were converted between the ages of 6 and 10.
- 20 percent came to Christ between the ages of 11 and 15.
- And 20 percent were saved at age 16 or later.

Eighty percent of the Christians in our church received Christ before age 16! And only 20 percent afterward.

Clearly, there is no magic age when a child is saved. It varies, like almost every child developmental issue. What then can a sensitive parent do to help their children discover the Lord in their own timing and at the appropriate age for them?

Expose

Expose children to the gospel. Paul reminded Timothy that from infancy, he had known the Holy Scriptures, "which are able to make you wise for salvation through faith which is in Jesus Christ" (2 Timothy 3:15). Today we have more Bible-related products for children than any other generation in history, and a visit to any Christian bookstore will provide a host of children's Bibles, devotional books, videos, cassettes, compact discs, maps, games, books, software, and puzzles. Select the ones you like best, and spend time with your child every day in Bible-learning activities and prayer.[5]

Tom and Laura set aside 10 minutes at bedtime each evening to read Scripture to their twins. Using a modern translation, they select easy-to-understand portions, read a few verses, and explain the meaning. Sometimes the boys read, sounding out words they don't know yet. Tom and Laura often ask their eight-year-olds a few questions to gage their attention and comprehension. "How old do you think the boy was who shared his lunch? How many baskets were left over?" Then the four bow their heads and pray. Sometimes one parent prays, sometimes they all pray around the circle. Sometimes the boys lead the prayers themselves. I'll not be surprised one day when both boys come to me, telling me that they have become Christians.

On the other hand, I know another family with parents so busy that family devotions are haphazard if not nonexistent.

They remind me of my tomato seedlings. Last spring I planted seeds in a flat of soil. They germinated and peeped through the dirt. But I was too busy to tend to them and didn't expose them to sufficient light. When a young tomato doesn't receive enough light, it reaches as high as it can, searching for the sun, becoming long, thin, stringy, and weak.

The same thing happens to children. They need constant exposure to the light of God's love and His Word, or they won't mature properly. So read the Bible to them. Go with them to Sunday School and church. Read them Christian books. Play Christian music. Let them see you pouring over the Word of God. Expose them to the gospel.

And pray.

And wait.

Never force or pressure children to receive Christ any more than you would pressure healthy plants to produce tomatoes. Just sow the seed and wait. Let the Holy Spirit cultivate His harvest.

But be alert to their questions and comments. Listen and watch for signs of germination. One day, in one way or another, that child will ask about becoming a Christian, and you move to the next step.

Explain

Explain the gospel as simply and clearly as you can. Years ago I wrote a simple explanation for John 3:16 that I've used in helping children come to Christ. I'm not suggesting you use this verbatim, but notice how simply the eternal truths of Scripture can be explained.

Who is God?
God is the person who made the heavens and the earth.
    He made light and night, land and sky, sun and moon.
        He made trees and plants. And bees and ants.
            And fleas and seas and knees and peas.
            And bumblebees and chimpanzees.
                He made everything. He even made you and me.
                The Bible says God loved the world.
What is the world?
 It is an enormous round ball, spinning in space, full of woods and waters.
    Fish and otters.
        Dogs and cats.
            Mice and rats.
                Birds and bats.
                    Flies and gnats.
                    And people.
Special people like you.
    God loves people like you very much.
        He loves you so much He has given you a special gift.
        His one and only Son.

Who is God's Son?

God's Son is Jesus, born on Christmas Day in a barn in Bethlehem.

He was wrapped in rags and laid in a heap of hay.

Jesus grew up in the little town of Nazareth.

He helped His mother Mary clean house.

He helped Joseph build furniture.

He studied in the school.

And splashed in the stream.

He played in the park.

And prayed in the church.

He never disobeyed His parents.

Or lost His temper.

Or hurt a friend.

He never cheated. He never lied.

He was perfect. Perfectly perfect.

When Jesus was thirty years old, He left Nazareth.

He traveled from town to town,

Walking and talking,

Teaching and preaching.

He stilled the storms and healed the sick.

He amazed the crowds and raised the dead.

But one day some evil people captured Jesus.

They made fun of Him.

They tied Him up.

And beat Him up.

They nailed His hands and feet to a cross-shaped post.

They wanted to kill Him.

They did kill Him.

They laughed as He died.

His friends took Him from the cross.

They buried Him in a cave.

He wasn't breathing.

He wasn't moving.

His heart was stopped.

His eyes were closed.

He was dead. Perfectly dead.

But He didn't stay that way! Three days later, the cave was empty.

Jesus was alive again!

His eyes were open.

His heart was beating.

His lungs were breathing.

He returned to life!

Why did Jesus die and return to life?

… that whoever believes in Him shall not perish.

Why would we perish?

Because we have all broken God's rules in the Bible.

We disobey our parents.

We lose our temper.

We hurt our friends.
We cheat.
We lie.
We are not perfectly perfect.

Since Jesus died on the cross, God can forgive us for not being perfect. He can forgive us for breaking His rules in the Bible. Then we can go to His perfect place. We can live in His happy home.

How do we receive this gift?
We believe in Him.
What does it mean to believe in Him?
It means...
to believe that He was born in Bethlehem.
to believe that He died and returned to life.
to believe that He can forgive us for disobeying God.
It means...
to believe it enough to obey Him.
to believe it enough to talk to Him in prayer.
It means...
to pray something like this:
Dear God, I believe that Jesus died and rose again. Please forgive me for breaking Your rules in the Bible. Help me obey You. I want Jesus to be my best friend. I want to live one day in Your happy land.

Scripture Search: **Look up the following Bible verses and fill in the blanks.**

Romans 3:23: For all have _____ and fall short of the glory of God.

Romans 6:23: For the wages of sin is _____ but the _____ of God is eternal life in Christ Jesus our Lord.

Romans 5:8: God demonstrated his own love for us in this: While we were still sinners _____ _____ for us.

Romans 10:9,13: If you confess with your mouth, "Jesus is Lord," and believe in your heart that God raised him from the dead, you will be _____ ... for, "Everyone who calls on the name of the Lord will be saved."

These four passages have been called the "Roman Road of Salvation." Suppose you had explained these verses to a person who is now ready to become a Christian. Based on these verses, compose a simple prayer he could use in asking Christ to become his Lord and Savior. Make it simple enough for your child to use. Use any terminology you'd like; there isn't a preset formula. Just explain as simply as you can the wonderful message of the gospel. Then ask your child to explain it back to you. Her ability or inability to articulate the gospel provides significant information as to whether she is ready to become a Christian. But if she is, help her offer a simple prayer similar to the one above.

Express

When your children ask Christ into their hearts, write down the date and the occasion in a treasured place, and let them sign their names to it. Many Christians feel a little disturbed later in life if they can't remember the exact time and place of their conversion. So record this benchmark in your child's history.

It's also important for your child to share with a close friend or relative his decision. Some churches provide such an opportunity. My church, for example, invites parents and children to the altar railing at the close of our Sunday services, and I introduce the child to the congregation as a new believer.

Baptism is another deeply significant way for your child to express openly his new relationship with Christ. If a child doesn't publicly acknowledge his new allegiance to Christ, he may doubt or devalue it when the new wears off.

I'm Still Not Sure What to Say to My Child

Perhaps you still feel insecure about leading your child to Christ. While you can always take your youngster to visit a Christian pastor, this is a tender and precious parenting moment that you shouldn't quickly delegate to another. Remember that the Holy Spirit is doing the real work of conversion in your child's heart. He is more concerned about your child's spiritual experience than you are, and He will help you. It's hard to botch the job when the Lord is involved!

One of the most ill-advised attempts at child conversion I've ever read about occurred when an elderly woman watched children playing in the streets outside her window in Aberdeen, Scotland. She grew concerned for their souls and longed to tell them of salvation. One dark afternoon she invited them into her small house, around her fire, and using the fire for her text, she bluntly told the children that if they didn't receive Christ as Savior they would burn in the fires of hell forever.

That isn't the approach I advocate for any reason, but one of the wide-eyed children, a little girl named Mary Slessor, gave her heart to Jesus that day. She became one of the most colorful and courageous missionaries in all church history, the "missionary heroine of Calabar."

We live in a world of strange values. We wear ourselves out to provide our child's material comfort, educational opportunities, and athletic achievement. But the greatest thing we ever do for our children is introduce them to the Master.

I love the story of the early American preacher David Marks. He died when he was only 40, his body exhausted from extreme labors for Christ. As he lay on his deathbed, he longed to preach one more sermon. The doctor forbade it, but Marks insisted. He had himself carried in a chair to a little schoolhouse near his home to talk to the children who were warned that Marks would probably die during the sermon and to remain calm! But Marks survived the trip, telling the children:

> *Forty years since my existence began. Then my mother, now a saint in glory, consecrated me to God. With earnest prayers she besought the Lord that I might be converted early in life, and often have I heard her speak of the place and of the time when she first obtained the witness of the Spirit that her prayers were answered. Often would she take me to the bedchamber—the warm tears would fall on my cheek—and she would tell me about the promise of God, on which her faith took hold, and would plead with me to give my heart and voice to the Savior. At the age of ten years I was converted, and at fifteen I felt that I was called to preach the gospel of Christ.[6]*

That's the top priority of parenting—to lead our kids to the King, for He died for each one of them.

> *And none of the ransomed ever knew*
> *How deep were the waters crossed*
> *Nor how dark was the night*
> *That the Lord passed through*
> *Ere He found His sheep that was lost.*
> *Out in the desert He heard its cry*
> *Sick and helpless and ready to die.*
>
> *But all through the mountains, thunder-riven,*
> *And up from the rocky steep*
> *There arose a glad cry*
> *To the gate of heaven,*
> *Rejoice I have found my sheep!*
> *And the angels echoed around the throne*
> *Rejoice for the Lord brings back His own.*

"Just so," Jesus said, "it is not my Father's will that even one of these little children should perish" (Matthew 18:14).

 ## P.S. (Practical Suggestions from Chapter 13)

1. Begin the habit of praying regularly for your child's conversion.

2. Select a church that places appropriate emphasis on evangelism. Talk with the children's minister about children and salvation.

3. Read to your child frequently from the four Gospels.

4. Visit the children's section in a Christian bookstore and note the variety and quality of Christian books, games, tapes, and videos. Purchase those that are appropriate for your child.

5. Learn how to lead someone to Christ. Ask your church if they provide such training. If not, call other churches and ask about short-term classes you can take. Ask in a Christian bookstore for evangelism materials.

6. When your child receives Christ as Savior, make it a memorable event and record it in a permanent place.

---

[1] David Shibley, "Why Child Evangelism Is Valid," *Moody,* April 1981, 27.

[2] Bruce Shelley, *Church History in Plain Language* (Waco: Word, 1982), 52.

[3] Paul Lee Tan, *Encyclopedia of 7,700 Illustrations: Signs of the Times* (Rockville, MD: Assurance, 1979), 233.

[4] Julia H. Johnston, *Fifty Missionary Heroes Every Boy and Girl Should Know* (New York: Revell), 125-126.

[5] See the author's book of devotions for families with young children, *Tiny Talks with God* (Nashville: Thomas Nelson, 1996). Other family devotional resources include *The Family Devotional Bible* published by Broadman & Holman; *Bible Express,* a devotional guide for children; and *Open Windows,* a daily devotional guide, all of which can be ordered from the Baptist Sunday School Board, 1-800-458-2772.

[6] Marilla Marks, ed., *Memoirs of the Life of David Marks, Minister of the Gospel,* (Dover, N.H.: The Free-Will Baptist Printing Establishment, 1847), 482.

Home Free!

Yes, [sigh] I know. You still have lots of questions. You're finding mountains, valleys, twists, and turns that weren't in this guide-book.

Well, I'll leave you with this: Perhaps the greatest secret about Christian parenting is that we're unable to do it. We can't live it in our own strength or by our own power. But when we're yielded to Christ, the Holy Spirit lives the Christ-life through us.

That means that Jesus Christ strengthens our parenting skills as we walk with Him.

Ephesians 5:18 commands, "Be filled with the Spirit." Then the Lord provides a list of effects: Spirit-filled people sing and make music in their hearts to the Lord. Spirit-filled couples have submissive attitudes toward one another. Spirit-filled husbands love their wives. Spirit-filled children obey their parents. And, in Ephesians 6:4, Spirit-filled parents raise their kids "in the training and instruction of the Lord."

So let Christ parent through you.

Display Christ's attitudes. Love His Word. Ask Him for His wisdom when you don't know what to do. Trust Christ with the results. Relax. And enjoy the trip.

That is empowered parenting.

Empowered Parenting Leader Guide

This Leader Guide was designed for you to use as you meet with other parents to review the material in *Empowered Parenting*. Gather with 12 to 15 parents from your church or community in a home, school, or church. Meet once each week for eight weeks and use the following plans.

Session 1
Review of the Introduction and Chapter 1

Group participants should receive this book before the first session with instructions to read the introduction and first chapter. The following lesson plans assume that parents will study the assigned material in advance.

This session (1) acquaints participants with each other fostering a climate of fellowship; and (2) introduces three foundational patterns for biblical parenthood, based on Deuteronomy 6.

Opening Activity

Help group members know each other better. Allow each participant to tell their names, where they grew up, and how many children they have. Remind members of the author's story in the Introduction about screaming over the cereal. Ask for volunteers to share similar "I blew it" stories. Then say: *"Parenting may be the most important obligation we face, and we've all occasionally blown it. None of us are prepared for it, and babies don't come with preprinted instructions tattooed on their bellies. But 2 Timothy 3:16-17 says, 'All Scripture is God-breathed and is useful for teaching, rebuking, correcting, and training in righteousness, so that the man of God may be thoroughly equipped for every good work.' Parenting is very 'good work!' This verse promises that God's Word can thoroughly teach and train us to be good parents. That belief is the thesis for this course."*

Content Overview

Encourage the group to locate the elements on the Learning Map that illustrate the material in the first chapter. Ask and discuss: *"What is significant about this location on the map?"* Work through the chapter, guiding the group to the three vital patterns for effective parenting. Use the Let's Talk and Scripture Search segments for discussion.

Closing Activity

Encourage participants to choose action steps they can take during the coming week to implement a truth discovered in unit 1. The P.S. segment lists good options; but let parents pose their own "practical suggestions" for applying what they've learned. Share in pairs, letting each share his or her action step with the other. Encourage participants to pair with someone other than their spouses. Be sensitive to any parents who need to commit their lives to Christ and begin praying for them privately. Close the time in prayer.

Looking Ahead

Point to the elements on the Learning Map to be covered in the next session. Encourage participants to read the material and complete all the learning activities.

Session 2
Review of Chapters 2, 3, and 4

This session discusses the context for child-raising. We don't parent in a vacuum. The quality of our parenting can't rise higher than its surrounding atmosphere. This lesson aims to strengthen the undergirding relationships of the home. In two-parent families, the marriage or remarriage is the core relationship. Single parents need a different set of partners—God, self, and vibrant Christian friends. Plan to customize this session to the particular needs in your group. However, don't miss the opportunity for parents in different home situations to better know and understand the homes of others. All three chapters stress the need for Christian friends and churches to support parents. Help your group to accept this group time as both a privilege for themselves and a responsibility to others.

Opening Activity
Have group participants locate the toll booths for today's session on the Learning Map. In threes, have them discuss one advantage and one disadvantage of their particular booth. Note that all three booths feed onto the same path. Encourage participants to discuss the significance of that.

Content Overview
Work through the content. Remember, once-married couples need to understand the burdens (and blessings) of single parents, and stepparents need to know the five stages of marriage in chapter 2. Here is the place to customize the session to your particular group and its needs. Use the Let's Talk and Scripture Search segments for discussion.

Options
Before the session, enlist three participants to facilitate a small group discussion—one for each chapter. During the session, allow group members to choose the group discussion they most want to join or the one that best fits their parenting situation.

Or, give members note cards for listing the three topics of greatest interest to them from these three chapters. Quickly compile results (during the opening activity) and lead a discussion on the topics of most interest to the group.

Closing Activity
Encourage participants to adopt action steps for the coming week and write them in the P.S. segments. End by saying *"Many times we're troubled by our homes or circumstances, but we often have more blessings than we acknowledge. Tonight we're going to end by praying sentence praises. You can pray as often as you'd like, and we'll pray in no particular order. The only rule is that you keep each prayer to one sentence beginning with the words, 'Thank you, Lord, for ... ' "*

Looking Ahead
Point out the next stops on the Learning Map: parenting during the prebirth period and the preschool years. Encourage participants to read the material and complete the learning activities.

Session 3
Review of Chapters 5 and 6

This session describes the challenges and joys of pregnancy and of parenting preschoolers. Assure class participants of this material's value for all parents. It will better prepare them to counsel and encourage expectant and new parents, to understand preschoolers, and to enjoy grandparenting!

Opening Activity
Locate the appropriate illustrations in the upper left corner of the Learning Map. Ask members to pair up with someone they've not been with in previous sessions and share one funny moment during pregnancy (theirs or their spouse's) or in parenting a preschooler. Call the group together and hear the ones from pairs where laughter was loudest.

Content Overview
Review the story of Zechariah and Elizabeth, directing the group to the three levels of prenatal parenting The issue of abortion may be raised. Be careful,to emphasize the primary purpose of the course—to empower parents in their child rearing skills. Then point out the *A, B, C, D,* and *E* of raising preschoolers on the Learning Map. Ask participants to choose one of the five letters, the one associated with positive memories during their preschool years. Group with others who choose the same letter. Allow groups to discuss key insights from their particular section of chapter 6. Hear reports from each group. As appropriate, use the Let's Talk and Scripture Search sections during the discussion.

Closing Activity
Chapter 6 mentions doing "prayer-a-phrasing," that is, converting Scripture passages into prayers for our children. Divide participants into groups of two or

three to share the prayers they composed from Scripture on page 64 for their children. Close in prayer in small groups or by asking one participant to lead in a Scripture prayer for the parents in the group.

Looking Ahead

Point to the elements on the Learning Map to be covered in the next session. Encourage participants to read the material and complete all the learning activities.

Session 4
Chapters 7 and 8

This session covers parenting elementary children and teens. You may want to devote more attention to one or the other, depending on the composition of your group. Remember that the material in all chapters contains important principles and practical insights transferable to other parenting stages. Also, truths learned in advance of the need may derail problems on the tracks up ahead.

Opening Activity

Direct the group to the Learning Map. Review the progress of the journey thus far and discuss the symbols appropriate to chapters 7 and 8. Invite volunteers to answer the initial Let's Talk question on page 72. Ask and discuss: *"Which, if any, of the five code words you see on the map—respect, discipline, encourage, teach, love—were a part of your elementary school years?"*

Content Overview

Use insights gained from sharing in the opening activity to finish discussion of chapter 7. Have members turn to page 77 and read the Scripture Search activity, beginning with the Scripture itself as a choral reading. Ask and discuss: *"How does this description of a loving parent impact your self-concept as a parent?"* Allow such sharing times to develop the tone of a support group, with members encouraging and giving insight to one another as they interact with the material.

Prepare and give a mini-lecture explaining how to "horizontalize," based on chapter 8. In threes, have members identify one of the five suggestions on horizontalizing that is, or will be, most difficult for them to implement. If time permits, share several answers with the large group.

Closing Activity

Use the P.S. segments to remind participants to take practical parenting in the coming week. Form a circle with your group. Ask participants willing to do so to offer one brief prayer request. As a request is made, ask for a volunteer willing to pray out loud about that request.

Looking Ahead

The next session deals with a subject perplexing to most parents–discipline. Locate the symbols on the Learning Map that are used to identify discipline in parenting. Encourage participants to read the material and complete all the learning activities.

Session 5
Review of Chapter 9

This session is always timely—disciplining children. It seems to be the toughest aspect of parenting and the one where marriage partners find themselves most in disagreement. This session can't resolve all differences! It can, however, stress the importance of discipline and offer practical techniques for it. If differences arise during group discussion, smile and handle them calmly, continually pointing the group to the biblical basis.

Opening Activity

On the Learning Map, discipline is symbolized by guard rails. Ask and discuss, *"Why was this symbol chosen."* Then ask volunteers to describe a disciplinary situation in their home. Make them brief. List these on a chalkboard or large sheet of paper.

Content Overview

With the list as a backdrop and touch point, survey chapter 9, beginning with the importance of discipline and the guidelines for discipline. Review the seven techniques by asking members to list them in their order of preference. Discuss these rankings. Be sure to use this opportunity to stress the importance of knowing your child in choosing disciplinary techniques. The discussion will probably flow easily, so reliance on the Scripture Search and Let's Talk segments may be less than in previous sessions.

Closing Activity

Break into pairs, giving participants a few minutes to share prayer requests relating to today's lesson. Encourage them to write down these requests and keep them in confidence. Ask them to pray for each other every day for the next week. Close in prayer.

Looking Ahead

Your participants were probably acutely aware of the discipline issues they face in being a parent. Perhaps not as obvious is the secret battle each one is fighting–fatigue. Locate the worn-out, worn-down father on the park bench (upper center edge on the Learning Map). Encourage participants to read the material and complete the learning activities so they can learn how to never feel or look this way.

Session 6
Review of Chapter 10

This session addresses a critical problem faced by modern parents—over-commitment and fatigue. Our fast-paced society with its multiple opportunities, demands, and around-the-clock schedules leaves little time for family interaction and little energy for quality relationships. Many parents suffer a sense of hopelessness from the financial pressures driving them to work long hours. The goal of this session is to lead participants (1) to evaluate their priorities and commitments, their personal schedules, and their time management patterns in light of biblical values; and (2) to take some action to relieve themselves of unnecessary stress.

Opening Activity

Use the Learning Map to review the parenting stages covered in *Empowered Parenting*. Ask and discuss: *"What contributes to parental fatigue in each of these stages?"*

Content Overview

Ask participants to think about a typical day in their family. Invite two volunteers to briefly share what goes on in their family. Say, *It makes me tired just hearing about it.* Discuss the Let's Talk question on page 104. Then, make sure participants understand the code words *scan, ban, can, and plan.* Divide into four equal groups and assign one word to each group. Instruct them to write an advertising slogan that would inspire parents to scan, ban, can, and plan fatigue out of their lives. Share slogans with the large group.

Closing Activity

Ask participants to choose one action step they will take immediately to reduce stress and create more quality time with the Lord, for themselves, and for their family. Consult the P.S. segment for ideas. Have participants share their steps in the four small groups. Close by offering a prayer for the group based on the Psalm 90 passage cited in the chapter.

Looking Ahead

Ask members to find the elements on the Learning Map about Scripture memory and the spiritual nurture of children. Impress on them the importance of the next part of the book. Encourage participants to read chapters 11 and 12 and complete all the learning activities.

Session 7
Review of Chapters 11 and 12

This session deals with two subjects that seem unrelated at first glance. They aren't. Scripture memory (chapter 11) can help prevent problems and provide comfort to the parents described in chapter 12. If your group is primarily the parents of younger children, you might want to focus mainly on chapter 11. If you have more parents of teenagers, you may want to spend more time on chapter 12.

Opening Overview

Based on your newspaper's current TV section, devise a TV trivia game. Ask questions about programs on your local stations. Let members compete for points, even prizes. Then ask the Let's Talk questions on page 112 about the role of television in their home. Discuss the dangers of unwholesome influences on our children's minds Challenge members to spot some symbolized on the Learning Map. Then discuss the benefits of Scripture memory. Brainstorm ideas for establishing Scripture memory patterns in participants' homes. Transition to chapter 12 by saying: *"Even after doing our best, we may still have problems with our children. The Bible is filled with stories of good people with troubled kids, and in Luke 15 we have an excellent case study."* Read aloud Ruth Graham's poem on page 127 and ask: *"What word or phrase most catches your attention in this poem? Why?"* Be sensitive to hurting parents in the group. Allow those willing to share their burdens with the group. Offer hope, and encourage each participant to implement the six steps described in the chapter.

Closing Activity

End this session with group prayer for hurting parents and their children. Give parents enough time to share their concerns, but do not allow this to become longer than necessary. Also, challenge parents to agree to lead their families to memorize one Bible verse in the coming week, choosing a verse from chapter 11's P.S. segment. Share verses in pairs. Encourage partners to hold each other accountable during the week.

Looking Ahead

Point to the cross on the Learning Map which will be covered in the final session. Encourage participants to read the material in chapter 13 and complete the learning activities.

Witnessing is involved—witnessing for Christ in an informal, protracted family setting. Your goal as group leader is to heighten awareness of the need and guide parents to develop the appropriate techniques of leading children to Christ. Don't become mired in debates about how old a child must be to become a Christian. The father or mother of the next John Wesley or Billy Graham may be in your group, so encourage participants to be committed to the spiritual nurture of their children.

Opening Activity

This is your last opportunity to study the Learning Map with your participants. Every major element of all 13 chapters of *Empowered Parenting* is visualized on this drawing. Briefly trace the journey and direct your participants to the cross. Then ask volunteers to tell how they became Christians.

Content Overview

Lead the group through the three steps described in chapter 13: *expose, explain, express*. Be sensitive to the possibility that some of the group members may not be Christians. This is your opportunity to witness for Christ! Use the Let's Talk and Scripture Search segments for discussion purposes. Conclude the session by asking for testimonies from those who have led their children to Christ or who were led to Christ as children by their parents.

Closing Activity

Because of the personal nature of parenting, it's likely that your group has bonded together. Spend time this last session in one group or in sub-groups praying for each other and for each other's children. Encourage participants to stay in touch with one another and pray for each other in the coming weeks and months.

Session 8
Review of Chapter 13

This session encourages parents to take an active role in leading their children to faith in Jesus Christ.

CHRISTIAN GROWTH STUDY PLAN

Preparing Christians to Serve

In the **Christian Growth Study Plan (formerly Church Study Course),** this book *Empowered Parenting: Raising Kids in the Nurture and Instruction of the Lord* is a resource for course credit in the subject area Home/Family of the Christian Growth category of diploma plans. To receive credit, read the book, complete the learning activities, show your work to your pastor, a staff member or church leader, then complete the following information. This page may be duplicated. Send the completed page to:

**Christian Growth Study Plan
127 Ninth Avenue, North, MSN 117
Nashville, TN 37234-0117
FAX: (615)251-5067**

For information about the Christian Growth Study Plan, refer to the current Christian Growth Study Plan Catalog. Your church office may have a copy. If not, request a free copy from the Christian Growth Study Plan office (615/251-2525).

Empowered Parenting: Raising Kids in the Nurture and Instruction of the Lord
COURSE NUMBER: CG- 0202
PARTICIPANT INFORMATION

Social Security Number	Personal CGSP Number*	Date of Birth

Name (First, MI, Last) ☐Mr. ☐Miss ☐Mrs. ☐		Home Phone

Address (Street, Route, or P.O. Box)	City, State	Zip Code

CHURCH INFORMATION

Church Name

Address (Street, Route, or P.O. Box)	City, State	Zip Code

CHANGE REQUEST ONLY

☐Former Name

☐Former Address	City, State	Zip Code

☐Former Church	City, State	Zip Code

Signature of Pastor, Conference Leader, or Other Church Leader	Date

*New participants are requested but not required to give SS# and date of birth. Existing participants, please give CGSP# when using SS# for the first time. Thereafter, only one ID# is required. *Mail To:* Christian Growth Study Plan, 127 Ninth Ave., North, MSN 117, Nashville, TN 37234-0117. Fax: (615)251-5067